The Daily Telegraph
BIG BOOK OF
QUICK
CROSSWORDS
8

The Daily Telegraph

BIG BOOK OF
QUICK
CROSSWORDS
8

PAN BOOKS

First published 2002 by Pan Books
an imprint of Pan Macmillan Ltd
Pan Macmillan, 20 New Wharf Road, London N1 9RR
Basingstoke and Oxford
Associated companies throughout the world
www.panmacmillan.com

In association with *The Daily Telegraph*

ISBN 978-0-330-49016-0

A CIP catalogue record for this book is available from
the British Library.

Image setting and design by Michael Mepham, Frome, Somerset
Printed and bound in Great Britain by Mackays of Chatham plc,
Chatham, Kent

Visit **www.panmacmillan.com** to read more about all our books and to buy
them. You will also find features, author interviews and news of any author
events, and you can sign up for e-newsletters so that you're always first to hear
about our new releases.

The Puzzles

Across

1 Hacking (8)
7 Musical exercise (5)
8 Credit facility (9)
9 Mineral spring (3)
10 Brad (4)
11 Energetic (6)
13 Compendium (6)
14 Puzzle (6)
17 Hebrew prophet (6)
18 Bob (4)
20 Manage (3)
22 Complex (9)
23 Sceptic (5)
24 All the gods (8)

Down

1 Comic entertainer (5)
2 Aperture (7)
3 Treads softly (4)
4 Shade of meaning (6)
5 Execrate (5)
6 Sudden collapse (7)
7 Professionally moral (7)
12 Mohammedan (7)
13 Crane (7)
15 Abandon (7)
16 Hindu psalm (6)
17 Senseless (5)
19 Song of praise (5)
21 Fissure (4)

2

Across

7 Burn (6)
8 Scarcity (6)
10 Distant past (4,3)
11 Banish (5)
12 Individually (4)
13 Tree (5)
17 Wide (5)
18 Threesome (4)
22 Wading bird (5)
23 Lawn game (7)
24 Meal (6)
25 Monetary unit (6)

Down

1 Prayer book (7)
2 Join (7)
3 Fragment (5)
4 Scheming woman (7)
5 Rubbish (coll) (5)
6 Mollusc (5)
9 Swiss lake (9)
14 Rope-shaped biscuit (7)
15 Distress (7)
16 Stance (7)
19 Animal (5)
20 Fruit (5)
21 Drive (5)

Across

1 Ecclesiastical building (6)
4 Beauty queen (5)
8 Arabian gazelle (5)
9 Occupying little space (7)
10 Difficulty (7)
11 Intoxicating liquor (4)
12 Artificial hair (3)
14 Units of current (4)
15 Latvian capital (4)
18 Male pig (3)
21 Incline (4)
23 Umpire (7)
25 Admit (7)
26 Deduce (5)
27 Unclean (5)
28 Point the way (6)

Down

1 Cunning (6)
2 Official dress (7)
3 Pipe made of gourd (8)
4 Explosive weapon (4)
5 Let (5)
6 Force money from (6)
7 Propeller (5)
13 Obscene scribblings (8)
16 Long-necked animal (7)
17 Strengthened by struts (6)
19 Twelve dozen (5)
20 Polecat (6)
22 Collier (5)
24 Portrait painter (4)

4

Across

1 Distress (8)
7 Pointer (5)
8 Widespread (9)
9 Drunkard (3)
10 Daybreak (4)
11 Departure (6)
13 Ephemerid (6)
14 More frightful (6)
17 Mechanic (6)
18 Benefit (4)
20 Bitumen (3)
22 Cruel (9)
23 Amusing (5)
24 Offer (8)

Down

1 Working party (5)
2 Tracks (7)
3 Plan (4)
4 Flag (6)
5 144 (5)
6 Chirp (7)
7 Hyper-sensitivity (7)
12 Smudgy (7)
13 Breed of dog (7)
15 Ailment (7)
16 Fix (6)
17 Promenade (5)
19 Agave fibre (5)
21 Pace (4)

Across

1 Left out (6)
4 Dull pains (5)
8 Elk (5)
9 Difficult (7)
10 Nil (7)
11 Footwear (4)
12 Strike (3)
14 Edge (4)
15 Singer (4)
18 Pair (3)
21 Scheme (4)
23 Fur dealer (7)
25 Small house (7)
26 Species (5)
27 Beforehand (5)
28 Vigour (6)

Down

1 Instant (6)
2 Curtail (7)
3 Vision (8)
4 Peak (4)
5 Illicit spirits (5)
6 Sibling (6)
7 Branch (5)
13 Herb (8)
16 Slimmer (7)
17 Red Indian (6)
19 Tender (5)
20 Rapacious (6)
22 Subsequently (5)
24 Cautious (4)

6

Across

1 Redolence (5)
4 Allay (7)
8 Infinite (7)
9 Green turf (5)
10 Drying-cloth (5)
11 Ramble (7)
13 Newspaper piece (4)
15 Dross (6)
17 Large bottle (6)
20 Highway (4)
22 Upstart (7)
24 Man-servant (5)
26 Scottish port (5)
27 Generosity (7)
28 Plane's personnel (7)
29 Follow in order (5)

Down

1 Asylum (7)
2 Give dowry (5)
3 Latticework (7)
4 Take for granted (6)
5 Italian food (5)
6 Magic lamp owner (7)
7 Tree (5)
12 Girl's name (4)
14 Aquatic bird (4)
16 Blacksmith (7)
18 Contrary (7)
19 French painter (7)
21 Bandit (6)
22 Dance (5)
23 Anaesthetic (5)
25 City of W Yorkshire (5)

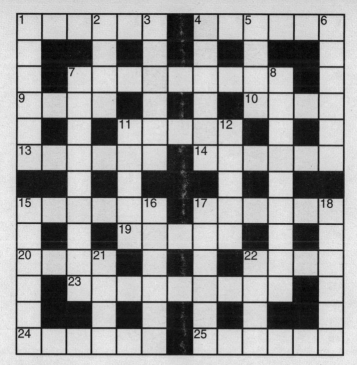

7

Across

1 Parisian tower (6)
4 Dormant (6)
7 Religious house (9)
9 Trudge (4)
10 Wharf (4)
11 Swiss financier (5)
13 Autocrat (6)
14 Serviette (6)
15 Diatribe (6)
17 Deadly (6)
19 Navigate (5)
20 Yobbo (4)
22 Haul (4)
23 Autograph (9)
24 Peasant (6)
25 Cure (6)

Down

1 Ran off to wed (6)
2 Victuals (4)
3 Ascertained (6)
4 Fall (6)
5 Aristocrat (4)
6 Ginger cake (6)
7 Abnormally large (9)
8 One-time Eng. county (9)
11 Personal property (5)
12 Avid (5)
15 Helm (6)
16 Of race (6)
17 Missive (6)
18 Bequest (6)
21 Shade (4)
22 Percussion instrument (4)

8

Across

1 Effervescent (5)
4 French port (6)
9 Vegetable (7)
10 Mother-of-pearl (5)
11 Tow (4)
12 Temporarily lost (7)
13 Month (3)
14 Conifer (4)
16 Peruvian Indian (4)
18 Fabulous bird (3)
20 Sketch (7)
21 English spa (4)
24 Song (5)
25 Copy (7)
26 Lass (6)
27 Lock of hair (5)

Down

1 False front (6)
2 Animal (5)
3 Period of time (4)
5 Coasting (anag.) (8)
6 Antiquated (7)
7 Fast (6)
8 Small crowbar (5)
13 Indifferent (8)
15 Meantime (7)
17 Laboured (6)
18 Allude (5)
19 Good health! (6)
22 Vigilant (5)
23 Irish pound (4)

Across

1 Loud (mus.) (5)
4 Robs (7)
8 Chirp (7)
9 Ring of target (5)
10 Overweight (5)
11 Resembling (7)
13 Deeds (4)
15 Afternoon nap (6)
17 Middle East area (6)
20 Pace (4)
22 Italian port (7)
24 Shiny fabric (5)
26 Foreigner (5)
27 Throb (7)
28 Refined molasses (7)
29 Dark period (5)

Down

1 Absurd (7)
2 European river (5)
3 Plead (7)
4 Push forward (6)
5 Form of speech (5)
6 Flavouring (7)
7 More certain (5)
12 Insular land (4)
14 Throw (4)
16 Imposing building (7)
18 Greek letter (7)
19 Line joining circle (7)
21 Side of head (6)
22 Characteristic (5)
23 Of sound (5)
25 Nasal accent (5)

10

Across

1 Stove (6)
4 Hole in the ground (6)
7 Laggard (9)
9 Lean (4)
10 Edge of pavement (4)
11 Dress (5)
13 Chased (6)
14 True (6)
15 Belgian port (6)
17 Bold (6)
19 American from a
  southern state (5)
20 Old Testament priest (4)
22 Non-flowering plant (4)
23 Try (9)
24 Get the better of (6)
25 Steps (6)

Down

1 Grasp (6)
2 Large oven (4)
3 Prize (6)
4 Ornamental pin (6)
5 Framework (4)
6 Marsupial (6)
7 Autograph (9)
8 Henceforth (9)
11 Pretence (5)
12 Muslim Scriptures (5)
15 Exaggerate (6)
16 Imperfection (6)
17 Wonder (6)
18 Cavalryman (6)
21 Afresh (4)
22 Kitty (4)

Across

1 Look hard (5)
4 Confederates (6)
9 Italian vermouth (7)
10 Cede (5)
11 Rock (4)
12 Natural environment (7)
13 Hard (3)
14 Entrance (4)
16 American state (4)
18 Obtain (3)
20 Affront (7)
21 Unlock (4)
24 Oscillate (5)
25 Imbibe (7)
26 Gleam (6)
27 Educator (5)

Down

1 Gloomy (6)
2 Concur (5)
3 Bad (4)
5 Idler (8)
6 Sluggishness (7)
7 Serene (6)
8 Vision (5)
13 Alien (8)
15 Songs (7)
17 Fragment (6)
18 Domestic fowl (5)
19 Reply (6)
22 Guide (5)
23 Treaty (4)

12

Across

1 Awaited arrival (6)
4 Routine tasks (6)
7 Artificial language (9)
9 Whirlpool (4)
10 Complacent (4)
11 Aquatic mammal (5)
13 Income (6)
14 Commotion (6)
15 Fur (6)
17 Sanity (6)
19 Card game (5)
20 Job (4)
22 Bucket (4)
23 Fool (9)
24 Prosper (6)
25 Italian painter (6)

Down

1 Right of entry (6)
2 Simple (4)
3 Agreement (6)
4 Swiss cottage (6)
5 Porridge ingredient (4)
6 Discourtesy (6)
7 Alpine plant (9)
8 Government referee (9)
11 Ship's lowest deck (5)
12 Sovereign (5)
15 Get the better of (6)
16 Tip over (6)
17 Modern (6)
18 Wrestling hold (6)
21 Flightless bird (4)
22 Mail (4)

Across

1 Fried potatoes (5)
4 Aircraft waiter (7)
8 Laborious (7)
9 Vacillate (5)
10 Glutted (5)
11 Intrinsic nature (7)
13 Merit (4)
15 Pace (6)
17 Maintenance (6)
20 Carousal (4)
22 Wane (7)
24 Mirthful (5)
26 On a par (5)
27 Huge (7)
28 Apparition (7)
29 Former Egyptian president (5)

Down

1 Wealthy Lydian king (7)
2 Sluggish (5)
3 Upbraided (7)
4 Sibling (6)
5 Distinctive disposition (5)
6 Loan (7)
7 Funereal chant (5)
12 Cosy (4)
14 Age (4)
16 Hermit (7)
18 Nightclothes (7)
19 Remuneration (7)
21 Purify (6)
22 Lees (5)
23 Fjord (5)
25 Ruled (5)

14

Across

1 Poultry bird (4)
3 Idiom (8)
9 Snow leopard (5)
10 Royal offspring (7)
11 Outfit (3)
13 Forerunner (9)
14 Small carnivore (6)
16 Rubbish (6)
18 Ruffian (9)
20 Zodiac sign (3)
22 Set apart (7)
23 Identical (5)
25 Edible jelly (8)
26 Good meal (4)

Down

1 Waste wool (5)
2 Succeed (3)
4 Fruit (6)
5 Heavy lace (7)
6 Lancaster (anag) (9)
7 Makes certain (7)
8 Jump (4)
12 Poisonous fungus (9)
14 Stuffer (7)
15 Tasteful (7)
17 Inn (6)
19 Finished (4)
21 Lubricated (5)
24 Employ (3)

Across

1 An eccentric (5)
4 Georgian composer (6)
9 Bright red (7)
10 Party with canned music (5)
11 Gentlewoman (4)
12 Pronounce forcibly (7)
13 Purchase (3)
14 Encourage (4)
16 Neat (4)
18 Professional charge (3)
20 Naval officer (7)
21 Competent (4)
24 Speedy (5)
25 Multiplied by three (7)
26 Motor (6)
27 Stratum (5)

Down

1 Fortress (6)
2 Grant (5)
3 Highland skirt (4)
5 Resign from throne (8)
6 Throw away (7)
7 Rifled (6)
8 Learn (5)
13 Fur helmet (8)
15 Playing boisterously (7)
17 Square-rigged vessel (6)
18 Woodwind (5)
19 Editorial article (6)
22 Intimidator (5)
23 In good health (4)

16

Across

1 Looked for (6)
4 Hurled (5)
8 Locust-tree (5)
9 Compartment (7)
10 Yacht race meeting (7)
11 Crier's call (4)
12 Precious stone (3)
14 Colonnade (4)
15 Metrical foot (4)
18 Boy (3)
21 Keep (4)
23 Delay (7)
25 Rogue (7)
26 Italian poet (5)
27 Watery discharge (5)
28 Parish officer (6)

Down

1 Safe (6)
2 Vertical (7)
3 Regular (8)
4 Musical instrument (4)
5 Unsteady (5)
6 Breathe audibly (6)
7 Lean animal (5)
13 Decide wrongly (8)
16 Grieved (7)
17 Razor (6)
19 Discourage (5)
20 Sternutation (6)
22 City in N France (5)
24 Tranquil (4)

Across

1 Gushing (7)
5 Metric weight (5)
8 Rub out (5)
9 Item (7)
10 Loquacious (9)
12 Mimic (3)
13 Spring festival (6)
14 Help (6)
17 Sport on snow (3)
18 Stupid (9)
20 Wash (7)
21 Curt (5)
23 Female relative (5)
24 Infinite (7)

Down

1 Cereal (5)
2 Pasture (3)
3 Repeat (7)
4 Free (6)
5 Name (5)
6 Juicy fruit (9)
7 Highest mountain (7)
11 Lethargy (9)
13 Greek letter (7)
15 Perfumed (7)
16 False (6)
18 Waterside plant (5)
19 Paces (5)
22 Fish-eggs (3)

18

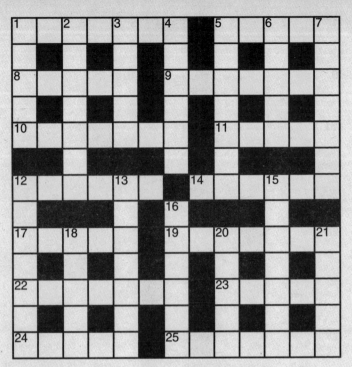

Across

1 Guarantee (7)
5 Large gulls (5)
8 Push lightly (5)
9 Warship (7)
10 Artery in neck (7)
11 Complete (5)
12 Grass-cutting implement (6)
14 One of *The Three Musketeers* (6)
17 Flower (5)
19 Prevalent in a district (7)
22 Esteems (7)
23 White-faced (5)
24 Bodily cavity (5)
25 Large hat (7)

Down

1 Go to pieces (5)
2 Hospital attendant (7)
3 Dormant (5)
4 Portuguese coin (6)
5 Amble (7)
6 Capsize (5)
7 Left over (7)
12 Outskirts (7)
13 Bone in arm (7)
15 Port in SW Tennessee (7)
16 Against (6)
18 Mus. instrument (5)
20 Adorn (5)
21 Principle (5)

Across

1 Police informer (5)
4 Itineraries (6)
9 Warlike (7)
10 Service chaplain (5)
11 Chances (4)
12 Frankness (7)
13 Vex (3)
14 Group of families (4)
16 Inquisitive (4)
18 Epileptic seizure (3)
20 Genuine (7)
21 Exploit (4)
24 Musical exercise (5)
25 Oyster plant (7)
26 Privateer (6)
27 Cloyed (5)

Down

1 Frolic (6)
2 Caustic (5)
3 Hide (4)
5 Adversary (8)
6 Wearisome (7)
7 Mountain range (6)
8 Mattress stuffing (5)
13 Unseemly (8)
15 Lethargy (7)
17 Slumbering (6)
18 Banquet (5)
19 Checked (6)
22 Victorian novelist (5)
23 Charitable donations (4)

20

Across

5 Sharp instrument (5)
8 Interrogate (8)
9 Shun (5)
10 Unquestioning (8)
11 Perfume (5)
14 Males (3)
16 Fruit (6)
17 Banish (6)
18 Moisture (3)
20 Jumped (5)
24 Month (8)
25 Unadorned (5)
26 Opening (8)
27 Light beer (5)

Down

1 Cephalopod (5)
2 Rhythm (5)
3 Undress (5)
4 Courteous (6)
6 Recommend (8)
7 Eastern (8)
12 Flower (8)
13 Precious stone (8)
14 Insane (3)
15 The present (3)
19 Not liable (6)
21 Unit of length (5)
22 Concerning (5)
23 Shakespearean spirit (5)

Across

7 Restaurant attendant (6)
8 Diminutive (6)
10 Hypodermic plunger (7)
11 Oil-producing fruit (5)
12 Spouse (4)
13 Scatter about (5)
17 Crazy (5)
18 Bottom of ship (4)
22 Additional (5)
23 Tell (7)
24 A tropic (6)
25 Weakly ineffectual (6)

Down

1 Pair (7)
2 Move to another land (7)
3 French river (5)
4 Bereaved husband (7)
5 Dignified (5)
6 Riotous fight (5)
9 Sympathetic feeling (9)
14 Administrator (7)
15 Not tense (7)
16 Swindled (7)
19 Light wall (5)
20 Unit of weight (5)
21 Trade (5)

22

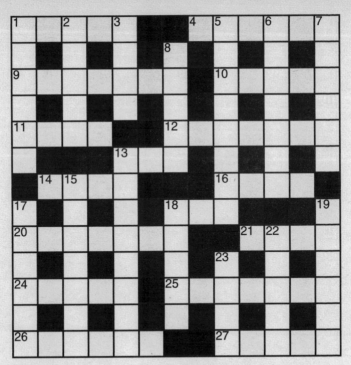

Across

1 Fetter (5)
4 German city (6)
9 Unaffected (7)
10 Dali Lama's land (5)
11 Nation (4)
12 Mixed in breed (7)
13 Steal (3)
14 Tub (4)
16 Soothe (4)
18 Baked dish (3)
20 Performance (7)
21 Competent (4)
24 Belonging to them (5)
25 Dramatic scene (7)
26 Discern (6)
27 Happening (5)

Down

1 Songbird (6)
2 Ancient Mexican (5)
3 Rule (4)
5 Ensnare (8)
6 Generous (7)
7 Provoke (6)
8 Vertical (5)
13 Oratory (8)
15 Very old (7)
17 Jarred on (6)
18 Planet (5)
19 Outcome (6)
22 Long note (mus.) (5)
23 Instrument (4)

Across

7 Breed of dog (6)
8 Sounded sad (6)
10 Late (7)
11 Portion (5)
12 Pleasant (4)
13 Normal (5)
17 Indicate (5)
18 Affection (4)
22 Danger (5)
23 Paradigm (7)
24 Italian city (6)
25 Wooded area (6)

Down

1 Astonish (7)
2 Expand (7)
3 Indigent (5)
4 Exhibit (7)
5 Applaud (5)
6 Viper (5)
9 Staff (9)
14 Miner (7)
15 Intricate (7)
16 Under (7)
19 Backbone (5)
20 Burst forth (5)
21 Boat (5)

Across

5 Strongbox (5)
8 Embellishment (8)
9 Lucid (5)
10 Fipple-flute (8)
11 New (5)
14 Peculiar (3)
16 Thrifty (6)
17 Choice (6)
18 Excavate (3)
20 Tingling (5)
24 Trachea (8)
25 Unbeliever (5)
26 Mining waste hill (8)
27 Utter (5)

Down

1 Stockpile (5)
2 Flair (5)
3 Simper (5)
4 Mean (6)
6 Merriment (8)
7 Photo (8)
12 Sweet-scented (8)
13 Uninformed (8)
14 Aged (3)
15 Pursue (3)
19 Hanging ice-spike (6)
21 Proverb (5)
22 French composer (5)
23 Lure (5)

Across

1 Elegiac poet (4)
3 High rank (8)
9 Corpulent (5)
10 French bean (7)
11 Titbit (3)
13 Get rid of (9)
14 Make fun of (6)
16 Frugality (6)
18 Protected (9)
20 Self-image (3)
22 Plaintive poet (7)
23 Meal (5)
25 Robing (8)
26 Merriment (4)

Down

1 Lustre (5)
2 Yes (3)
4 Goats' wool (6)
5 E Anglian city (7)
6 Hybrid fruit (9)
7 Implore (7)
8 Bazaar (4)
12 Keep on trying (9)
14 Inflate (7)
15 Particulars (7)
17 Native of Brittany (6)
19 Open valley (4)
21 Yellow-orange (5)
24 Zero (3)

26

Across

1 Cogitate (5)
4 Permitted (7)
8 Cookie (7)
9 Impressionist painter (5)
10 Meat cut (5)
11 Month (7)
13 Entice (4)
15 Bivalve (6)
17 Nothing (6)
20 Barrier (4)
22 Suffocate (7)
24 Fastener (5)
26 Drive out (5)
27 Diabetic drug (7)
28 Plan (7)
29 Water-lily (5)

Down

1 Hot pepper sauce (7)
2 Progeny (5)
3 Finger joint (7)
4 Writer (6)
5 Boundary (5)
6 Chatterer (coll.) (7)
7 Put off (5)
12 US money (4)
14 Press (4)
16 Constellation (7)
18 Air spray (7)
19 Lockjaw (7)
21 Painter (6)
22 eg Ewe (5)
23 Split in two (5)
25 Manservant (5)

Across

5 Rub finely (5)
8 Dirty (8)
9 Griddle cake (5)
10 Trustworthy (8)
11 Liberated (5)
14 Long period of time (3)
16 Defame (6)
17 Old policeman (6)
18 Female deer (3)
20 Thin finishing mortar (5)
24 Lost footing (8)
25 Perfect (5)
26 Detested thing (8)
27 Stream (5)

Down

1 Indian dish (5)
2 Fabric (5)
3 Film award (5)
4 Tradesman (6)
6 Wind instrument (8)
7 Offered (8)
12 Large dog (8)
13 Copy (8)
14 Conclusion (3)
15 Primate (3)
19 Trip (6)
21 Metal worker (5)
22 Slumber (5)
23 Concepts (5)

28

Across

1 Constellation (5)
4 Layering (7)
8 News (7)
9 Drunken spree (5)
10 Elf (5)
11 Information (3-4)
13 Chain of rocks (4)
15 Cambridge college (6)
17 Carnival (6)
20 Meat (4)
22 Word with same
   meaning (7)
24 Tibetan capital (5)
26 Groom (5)
27 Natural (7)
28 Long (7)
29 Dance (5)

Down

1 Sea-creature (7)
2 Forefinger (5)
3 Convent (7)
4 Struggle (6)
5 Arm joint (5)
6 Fiery (7)
7 Gather facts (5)
12 Dyke builder (4)
14 Covetousness (4)
16 Lamp (7)
18 Unlawful (7)
19 Corsican capital (7)
21 Incorporate (6)
22 Part of a flower (5)
23 Tenon (anag.) (5)
25 Part of Vietnam (5)

Across

1 Singers (5)
4 Masticated (6)
9 Archbishop (7)
10 Regretful (5)
11 Sea-eagle (4)
12 Very large (7)
13 Enthusiast (3)
14 Competent (4)
16 Ripped (4)
18 Enemy (3)
20 Book (7)
21 Cease (4)
24 Instrument (5)
25 Epicure (7)
26 Blush (6)
27 Rice-field (5)

Down

1 Metal (6)
2 Sea (5)
3 Back (4)
5 Pause (8)
6 Fighting man (7)
7 English poet (6)
8 Criminal (5)
13 Dreadful (8)
15 Bird (7)
17 Suitable (6)
18 Pretend (5)
19 Dispassion (6)
22 Faint-hearted (5)
23 Spring (4)

30

Across

1 Hillock (5)
4 Readable (7)
8 Keep up (7)
9 Colour (5)
10 Castigates (5)
11 Blackout (7)
13 Curse (4)
15 Scottish loch (6)
17 Brawl (6)
20 Nought (4)
22 Baffle (7)
24 Peruses (5)
26 Ballads (5)
27 Proposition to be proven (7)
28 Aberrant (7)
29 TRail (5)

Down

1 Small falcon (7)
2 Start (5)
3 Relationship (7)
4 Surgeon's knife (6)
5 Russian dramatist (5)
6 Small alarm (7)
7 Premium Bonds computer (5)
12 Fish (4)
14 Cutting tool (4)
16 Seafarer (7)
18 Penalty (7)
19 Face veil (7)
21 Outlandish (6)
22 Adhesive (5)
23 Composer (5)
25 Main artery (5)

Across

1 Lubricant (6)
4 Strength of spirit (5)
8 Worth (5)
9 Terse (7)
10 Merry-making (7)
11 Parched (4)
12 Pair of performers (3)
14 Soon (4)
15 Locate (4)
18 Glue (3)
21 Sepulchre (4)
23 Verbally insulting (7)
25 Ingenuous (7)
26 Requested (5)
27 Cavalry division (5)
28 Watchman (6)

Down

1 Rule (6)
2 Animate (7)
3 Of solid worth (8)
4 Concordat (4)
5 Possessor (5)
6 Outward appearance (6)
7 Welsh county (5)
13 Kiss (8)
16 Coppice (7)
17 Royal House (6)
19 Rectory (5)
20 Fatal (6)
22 Paris subway (5)
24 Seaweed (4)

32

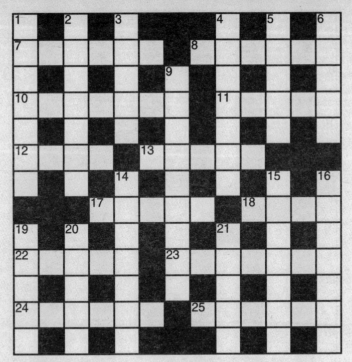

Across

7 Barrow-boy (6)
8 Sums up (6)
10 Spring flower (7)
11 Piebald horse (5)
12 Put (down) (4)
13 Colour (5)
17 Mohammed's birthplace (5)
18 Prophet (4)
22 Nut (5)
23 Gem (7)
24 Dapper (6)
25 Brandy (6)

Down

1 Shoulder-blade (7)
2 Pain-killer (7)
3 First appearance (5)
4 Intricate (7)
5 Senseless (5)
6 Race-course (5)
9 Diametric (anag.) (9)
14 Part of horse (7)
15 Echo (7)
16 Forecast (7)
19 Not these (5)
20 Blue (5)
21 Devastation (5)

Across

1 Gather (6)
4 Measure mass (5)
8 Perch (5)
9 Gaunt (7)
10 Generosity (7)
11 Cow shed (4)
12 Spinning toy (3)
14 Insect (4)
15 Engrossed in thought (4)
18 Japanese coin (3)
21 Grave (4)
23 Given confidence (7)
25 Three stanza poem (7)
26 Incompetent (5)
27 Mistake (5)
28 Fused together (6)

Down

1 Spirit of confidence (6)
2 Scottish pouch (7)
3 Petition (8)
4 Payment (4)
5 Med. country (5)
6 Played for time (6)
7 Card game (5)
13 Social standing (8)
16 Foreshadow (7)
17 Horse building (6)
19 Undressed (5)
20 Prepared for publication (6)
22 Tooth (5)
24 Animal's home (4)

34

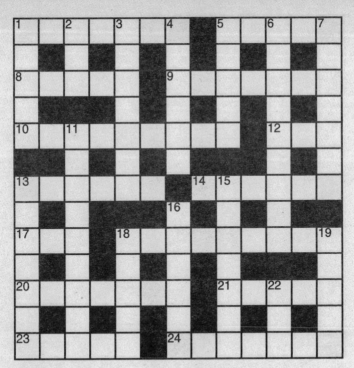

Across

1 Rock (7)
5 Peer (5)
8 Colour (5)
9 Apt to break (7)
10 Napkin (9)
12 Turkish commander (3)
13 Prairie-wolf (6)
14 End (6)
17 Indian rule (3)
18 Bird (9)
20 Forestall (7)
21 Revive (5)
23 Undraped (5)
24 Soldier (7)

Down

1 Sham (5)
2 Utilise (3)
3 Teeth expert (7)
4 Refund (6)
5 Din (5)
6 Military unit (9)
7 Humbug (7)
11 Icelandic capital (9)
13 Caricature (7)
15 Conflagration (7)
16 Customer (6)
18 Dignified (5)
19 Cutter (5)
22 Short sleep (3)

Across

1 Hee-haws (5)
4 Comprehends (5)
10 Hide (7)
11 Poetry (5)
12 Improve (5)
13 Tell (7)
15 Rim (4)
17 Gardening tool (5)
19 Egg-shaped (5)
22 Sea-eagle (4)
25 Hostilities (7)
27 Spherical (5)
29 Measuring device (5)
30 Free time (7)
31 Very pale (5)
32 Stem (5)

Down

2 Wash (5)
3 Ceded (7)
5 At no time (5)
6 Authorisation (7)
7 Fight (5)
8 Hold on (5)
9 Revolt (5)
14 Very long time (4)
16 Antlered beast (4)
18 Buccaneers (7)
20 Decision (7)
21 Bog (5)
23 Kingdom (5)
24 Viper (5)
26 Consent (5)
28 Normal (5)

Across

1 Aroma (5)
4 Kerry's county town (6)
9 Deep-seated (7)
10 Tenth (5)
11 Labour (4)
12 Abundant (7)
13 Misery (3)
14 Ashen (4)
16 Declare (4)
18 Mountain pass (3)
20 Consistent (7)
21 Footfall (4)
24 Stringed instrument (5)
25 Wrench (7)
26 Zone (6)
27 Recess (5)

Down

1 Bad writing (6)
2 Tree (5)
3 Diplomacy (4)
5 Sane (8)
6 Salad plant (7)
7 Devon city (6)
8 Slant (5)
13 Prosperous (4-2-2)
15 Cherubic (7)
17 Plant (6)
18 Collision (5)
19 Scattered (6)
22 Pick-me-up (5)
23 Farm building (4)

Across

5 Distribute (5)
8 Seers (8)
9 Exemplar (5)
10 Lengthen (8)
11 Fuse (5)
14 Meadow (3)
16 Dinner jacket (6)
17 Established practice (6)
18 Quoits target (3)
20 Total confusion (5)
24 Lawbreaker (8)
25 Delicate (5)
26 Gigantic (8)
27 Ottoman governor (5)

Down

1 Overturned (5)
2 Benefactor (5)
3 Old Tories' adversaries (5)
4 Sculpted figure (6)
6 Pleasure-seeker (8)
7 Response (8)
12 Feeling of well-being (8)
13 Destroy (8)
14 Abraham's nephew (3)
15 Winning service (3)
19 Straying (6)
21 Astute (5)
22 Irritate (5)
23 Go red (5)

38

Across

1 Professional (6)
4 Banter (5)
8 Perforations (5)
9 White ant (7)
10 Concise (7)
11 Fruit (4)
12 Greek island (3)
14 Soon (4)
15 Slight cough (4)
18 Beverage (3)
21 Hazard (4)
23 Sturgeon's roe (7)
25 Talk (7)
26 Ingrained dirt (5)
27 Fabric (5)
28 View (6)

Down

1 Breathe out (6)
2 Bird (7)
3 Vibrant (8)
4 Bitter sweet (4)
5 Copying (5)
6 Blinker (6)
7 Ship's funnel (5)
13 Las Vegas (anag.) (8)
16 Scrutinise (7)
17 Spring flower (6)
19 Oak seed (5)
20 Choose (6)
22 Elegant (5)
24 School (4)

Across

1 Observer (7)
5 Exmoor outlaw (5)
8 Fine clay deposit (5)
9 Acrid (7)
10 Genuineness (9)
12 Garden implement (3)
13 Entry (6)
14 Strong blue (6)
17 Stupid person (3)
18 Central computer circuit (9)
20 Middle Easterner (7)
21 Test metal (5)
23 Garden herb (5)
24 Air current (7)

Down

1 Principality (5)
2 Knot together (3)
3 Female entertainer (7)
4 Mend (6)
5 Fop (5)
6 Incidental expenses (9)
7 Plead (7)
11 Essential (9)
13 Extremely hard (7)
15 Perform surgery (7)
16 Woman's hat (6)
18 Amount asked (5)
19 Kingly (5)
22 Total (3)

40

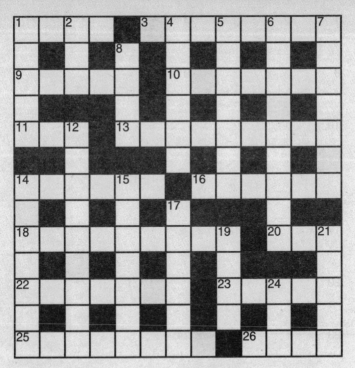

Across

1 Portion (4)
3 Feather-brushes (8)
9 Force back (5)
10 Gigantic (7)
11 Jump on one foot (3)
13 Investigator (9)
14 Fairly rough sea (6)
16 Wrench (6)
18 Esplanade (9)
20 Devour (3)
22 Of little importance (7)
23 Flinch (5)
25 Prominent feature (8)
26 Cattle (4)

Down

1 Make hot & dry (5)
2 Split (3)
4 Resident of an institution (6)
5 Marsh-marigold (7)
6 Disentangle (9)
7 Ship's doctor (7)
8 Dressed (4)
12 Advancement (9)
14 Chief city (7)
15 Reward (7)
17 Mariner (6)
19 Every (4)
21 Italian city (5)
24 Grow (3)

Across

1 Destroyed (7)
5 Type of window (5)
8 Surf (5)
9 Nasty (7)
10 Choosy (9)
12 Decay (3)
13 Titbit (6)
14 Expunge (6)
17 Donkey (3)
18 Self-assure (9)
20 Foliage (7)
21 Male singer (5)
23 Perfume (5)
24 Playhouse (7)

Down

1 Insects (5)
2 Flightless bird (3)
3 Patella (7)
4 Rubbish (6)
5 Egg-shaped (5)
6 Meddle (9)
7 Baby clothes (7)
11 Scenery (9)
13 White wine (7)
15 Letter (7)
16 Put in (6)
18 Map (5)
19 Trio (5)
22 Catch (3)

42

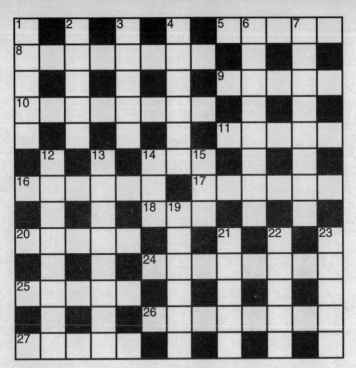

Across

5 Yells (5)
8 Gemstone (8)
9 Garden tool (5)
10 'Sticky' sweet! (8)
11 Bird (5)
14 Dripping (3)
16 Salad root (6)
17 Set aside (6)
18 Yelp (3)
20 Guide (5)
24 Firearm (8)
25 Flighty (5)
26 One who flees (8)
27 Sluggish (5)

Down

1 Devotional song (5)
2 Fruit (5)
3 Seat (5)
4 Furrow (6)
6 Obvious (8)
7 Insect (8)
12 Conjurer (8)
13 Confusion (8)
14 For what reason (3)
15 Gratuity (3)
19 Wide road (6)
21 Theme (5)
22 Shun (5)
23 Avidity (5)

Across

1 Sable (5)
4 Blasé (5)
10 Grumbler (7)
11 Upright (5)
12 Section (5)
13 Forbearing (7)
15 Become limp (4)
17 Brag (5)
19 Fails to include (5)
22 Ice cream (4)
25 Gratification (7)
27 Also-ran (5)
29 Scoundrel (5)
30 Infinite (7)
31 Emends text (5)
32 Set of twenty (5)

Down

2 Unshackled (5)
3 Nuts (7)
5 Vast sea (5)
6 Component part (7)
7 Open-mouthed (5)
8 Military exercises (5)
9 Condition (5)
14 Public school (4)
16 Irritation (4)
18 Indebted (7)
20 Tuneful (7)
21 Love deeply (5)
23 Aquatic mammal (5)
24 Alloy (5)
26 Distinguished (5)
28 Blaspheme (5)

44

Across

1 Placard (6)
4 Wide (5)
8 Governor (5)
9 Varied (7)
10 Fielding position (4-3)
11 Continent (4)
12 Newt (3)
14 Lake (4)
15 Ascent (4)
18 Twosome (3)
21 Rowing implements (4)
23 Agreement (7)
25 Rodent (7)
26 Knock over (5)
27 Spacious (5)
28 Quick look (6)

Down

1 Colour (6)
2 Noiselessness (7)
3 Signed on (8)
4 Flock (4)
5 Monsters (5)
6 Disc jockey (3-3)
7 Proverb (5)
13 Calm (8)
16 Ten-gallon hat (7)
17 Parent (6)
19 Yellow pigment (5)
20 Sculpture (6)
22 Young lover (5)
24 Support (4)

Across

1 Accomplice (7)
5 Measure on scales (5)
8 With more years (5)
9 Toady (7)
10 Wealth (9)
12 Indian district (3)
13 Musical note (6)
14 Fine building stone (6)
17 Suitable (3)
18 Everlasting (9)
20 White ant (7)
21 Darkness (5)
23 Royal family (5)
24 Gossip (7)

Down

1 Odour (5)
2 Conclude (3)
3 Inflict pain (7)
4 Fr. dramatist (6)
5 Make fabric (5)
6 Unreadable (9)
7 Pasturage (7)
11 Broken (9)
13 Group of four (7)
15 Opposed to (7)
16 Religious leader (6)
18 Earlier (5)
19 Teacher (5)
22 Semirigid colloid (3)

Across

1 Recognise (4)
3 Absurdity (8)
9 Brownish-yellow (5)
10 Chat (7)
11 Annoy (3)
13 Advantage (9)
14 Young cat (6)
16 Pursued (6)
18 Surgical treatment (9)
20 So far (3)
22 English cheese (7)
23 Practical joke (5)
25 Wisdom (8)
26 Hide (4)

Down

1 Gurkha knife (5)
2 Eggs (3)
4 Exotic flower (6)
5 Pig-like (7)
6 US state (3,6)
7 Intellectual (7)
8 Hobble (4)
12 Northants. town (9)
14 Ruined city in Crete (7)
15 Flexible (7)
17 Songbird (6)
19 Back of the neck (4)
21 Symbol (5)
24 Diving bird (3)

Across

1 Church minister (6)
4 Supernatural dwarf (5)
8 Scolded (5)
9 Remainder (7)
10 Devilish (7)
11 French cheese (4)
12 Finish (3)
14 Agitate (4)
15 Notion (4)
18 Desire (3)
21 Declare (4)
23 Beg (7)
25 Go on (7)
26 Silly (5)
27 Tend (5)
28 Belittle (6)

Down

1 Gathered skirt (6)
2 Try (7)
3 Usual (8)
4 Job (4)
5 Command (5)
6 German songs (6)
7 Cost (5)
13 Tirade (8)
16 Raise (7)
17 Moisten (6)
19 Indigent (5)
20 Scattered (6)
22 Smell (5)
24 Lake (4)

48

Across

1 Exhibits (5)
4 Opera hat (6)
9 Cheat (7)
10 Hot drink (5)
11 Fur (4)
12 Retribution (7)
13 Perceive (3)
14 Bucket (4)
16 Inquisitive (4)
18 Obese (3)
20 Do well (7)
21 N Indian city (4)
24 Make ashamed (5)
25 Bird (7)
26 Trashy (6)
27 For this reason (5)

Down

1 Plant (6)
2 Constellation (5)
3 Lather (4)
5 Greasy medication (8)
6 Flying horse (7)
7 Fight against (6)
8 French river (5)
13 Slovenly (8)
15 Alligator pear (7)
17 Utters (6)
18 New (5)
19 Fishing gear (6)
22 Very small amount (5)
23 Fable (4)

Across

1 Cascading (7)
5 Kingly rule (5)
8 Start again (5)
9 Tourist centres (7)
10 Pleasure-trip (9)
12 Joke (3)
13 Buff up (6)
14 Defective (6)
17 Flightless bird (3)
18 Explain, translate (9)
20 Marine bivalve (7)
21 Mental picture (5)
23 Clothe (5)
24 Imagined (7)

Down

1 Funds (5)
2 Large tea-container (3)
3 To the inside (7)
4 Alliacaeous plant (6)
5 Colophony (5)
6 Abnormal (9)
7 Posy (7)
11 Compute (9)
13 Gratified (7)
15 Flight company (7)
16 Slow-witted (6)
18 Wastes time (5)
19 General tendency (5)
22 Object (3)

50

Across

1 Sequence (5)
4 Reasonable (7)
8 Blissful state (7)
9 Aquatic carnivore (5)
10 Overturn (5)
11 European country (7)
13 Listed article (4)
15 Lessen (6)
17 Hinder (6)
20 Affectedly artistic (4)
22 Infuriate (7)
24 Jargon (5)
26 Deep sea (5)
27 Oozing (7)
28 German city (7)
29 Give way (5)

Down

1 Vanquish (7)
2 Troubles (5)
3 Stretchable (7)
4 Dislike intensely (6)
5 Snarl (5)
6 Small dwelling (7)
7 Sensational (5)
12 Exclude (4)
14 Durable wood (4)
16 BIshop's see (7)
18 Inexplicable event (7)
19 Betrothed (7)
21 Sanity (6)
22 High-minded (5)
23 Admitted (5)
25 Nimble (5)

51

Across

1 Captured (6)
4 Mucous (5)
8 Pungent vegetable (5)
9 Throat gland (7)
10 Condition (7)
11 Cure (4)
12 Louse egg (3)
14 Austen novel (4)
15 Animal's foot (4)
18 Stubby nosed dog (3)
21 Eastern staple (4)
23 Circus performer (7)
25 Approve (7)
26 Speak (5)
27 Spacious (5)
28 Protected from light (6)

Down

1 Rough at sea (6)
2 Regulation dress (7)
3 Disability (8)
4 Smell strongly (4)
5 Run away with (5)
6 Centre (6)
7 Cured pigmeat (5)
13 Assiduous (8)
16 Circled (7)
17 Alcoholic tonic (6)
19 Auctioneer's hammer (5)
20 Looked fixedly (6)
22 Main division of poem (5)
24 Small horse (4)

Across

1 Unit of heat (5)
4 Pastoral poem (5)
10 Rodent pet (7)
11 Plenty (5)
12 Bend (5)
13 French coin (7)
15 Very old (4)
17 Lessen (5)
19 Saying (5)
22 Capital city (4)
25 Predicament (7)
27 Depart (5)
29 Young eel (5)
30 Entrance (7)
31 Soil (5)
32 Aver (5)

Down

2 Greek poet (5)
3 Withdraw (7)
5 Sketched (5)
6 Peewit (7)
7 Outrage (5)
8 Pair (5)
9 At no time (5)
14 Dutch cheese (4)
16 Bacillus (4)
18 South American country (7)
20 Pleasure (7)
21 Viper (5)
23 Fertile spot (5)
24 Stop (5)
26 Deserve (5)
28 Representative (5)

53

Across

1 Manufacturer (5)
4 Seer (7)
8 Cocktail (7)
9 Cleanse (5)
10 Social class (5)
11 Small bone (7)
13 Canvas shelter (4)
15 Grasshopper (6)
17 Speaker (6)
20 Strip (4)
22 Man's name (7)
24 Jargon (5)
26 Accomplishing (5)
27 Irish county (7)
28 Chest of drawers (7)
29 Senior member (5)

Down

1 Harmonious (7)
2 Renown (5)
3 Disease (7)
4 Forgive (6)
5 Fertile spot (5)
6 Bean (7)
7 Board (5)
12 Cease (4)
14 English artist (4)
16 Narcotic drug (7)
18 Repeal (7)
19 Diet (7)
21 Fisherman (6)
22 Worn out (5)
23 Capital of Nigeria (5)
25 Deck (5)

54

Across

7 Church minister (6)
8 Joked (6)
10 Sure (7)
11 Guide (5)
12 Implement (4)
13 Regretful (5)
17 Holy man (5)
18 Grain store (4)
22 Expert (5)
23 Gemstone (7)
24 Gain (6)
25 Managing (6)

Down

1 Train (7)
2 Soldier (7)
3 Wanderer (5)
4 Sweet course (7)
5 Precipitous (5)
6 Decorate (5)
9 Meet (9)
14 Skipper (7)
15 Fairy queen (7)
16 Slavery (7)
19 Glad (5)
20 Devil (5)
21 Lawbreaker (5)

Across

1 Larger (6)
4 Avoided (6)
7 Racing dog (9)
9 Tiller (4)
10 Flightless bird (4)
11 Ewe (5)
13 Platform (6)
14 Sharp bend (3-3)
15 Gap (6)
17 Crustaceans (6)
19 Thump (5)
20 Cage (4)
22 Pain (4)
23 Fruit (9)
24 Hole in the ground (6)
25 Scribble (6)

Down

1 Senior cleric (6)
2 Bug (4)
3 Regular beat (6)
4 Tied up (6)
5 Submerge (4)
6 Bold (6)
7 Roman fighter (9)
8 Tact (9)
11 Dawn (3-2)
12 Cook slowly (5)
15 Feverish (6)
16 Meal (6)
17 Long speech (6)
18 Glacial epoch (3,3)
21 Agreement (4)
22 Jason's ship (4)

56

Across

1 Dutch cheese (5)
4 Get together (6)
9 Beaming (7)
10 Remains (5)
11 Certain (4)
12 Decaying (7)
13 Mother (3)
14 Create (4)
16 Land measure (4)
18 Write (3)
20 Lift (7)
21 Step (4)
24 Yell (5)
25 Instructor (7)
26 Stable (6)
27 Baby food (5)

Down

1 Showy (6)
2 Beneath (5)
3 Partly open (4)
5 Breed of dog (8)
6 Weightier (7)
7 Abdicate (6)
8 Tempest (5)
13 Left (8)
15 Impressive (7)
17 Population count (6)
18 Unimportant (5)
19 Litter (6)
22 Greenfly (5)
23 Equitable (4)

Across

1 Middle (6)
4 Conspicuous (6)
7 Got well again (9)
9 Rip (4)
10 Cleanse (4)
11 Roost (5)
13 Fortified dwelling (6)
14 Composer (6)
15 Inflame to action (6)
17 Walking poles (6)
19 Banish (5)
20 Wine dregs (4)
22 Unconscious state (4)
23 Subtraction (9)
24 Jumbled language (6)
25 Remove from office (6)

Down

1 Indo-European language (6)
2 Row (4)
3 Epic poem (6)
4 Bad odour (6)
5 Increased in size (4)
6 Deadly (6)
7 Plundered (9)
8 Garden weed (9)
11 Flat piece of metal (5)
12 Swiftness of action (5)
15 Wasting time (6)
16 Forgive (6)
17 Reprimanded (6)
18 In short supply (6)
21 Yugoslav (4)
22 Seizure of power (4)

58

Across

1 Hebridean island (5)
4 Pale (5)
10 Vernal —— (7)
11 Become one (5)
12 Old measure (5)
13 N American Indian (7)
15 Shallow container (4)
17 Eskimo house (5)
19 Gemstone (5)
22 Mediocre (2-2)
25 One more (7)
27 Indian prince (5)
29 Old-fashioned person (5)
30 Having claws (7)
31 W German port (5)
32 Ballroom dance (5)

Down

2 Firework (5)
3 Orange dye (7)
5 Hunting dog (5)
6 Copse (7)
7 Long seat (5)
8 Surplus (5)
9 Dog-like animal (5)
14 Unfledged hawk (4)
16 Flower (4)
18 US state (7)
20 Ape (7)
21 Israeli port (5)
23 Harangue (5)
24 Sinister (5)
26 Austrian composer (5)
28 Girl's name (5)

Across

1 Writer (6)
4 Wharves (5)
8 Packing-case (5)
9 Cost (7)
10 Gave (7)
11 Finest (4)
12 Agreement (3)
14 Mountain (4)
15 Notion (4)
18 Consume (3)
21 Always (4)
23 Intellectual (7)
25 Maybe (7)
26 Loose-limbed (5)
27 Upright (5)
28 Card-game (6)

Down

1 Comply (6)
2 Learner (7)
3 Pass (8)
4 Drugs (4)
5 Boat (5)
6 Afternoon rest (6)
7 Prepared (5)
13 Exceptional (8)
16 Chosen (7)
17 Persons (6)
19 Laconic (5)
20 Stick (6)
22 Weird (5)
24 Final (4)

60

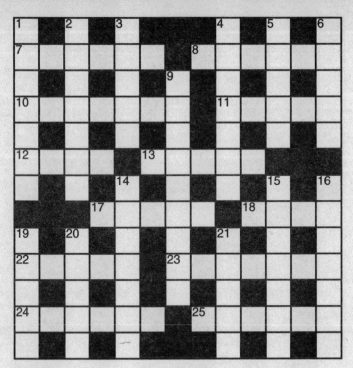

Across

7 German poet (6)
8 Fires (6)
10 Put in danger (7)
11 Panorama (5)
12 Elephant's tooth (4)
13 Propeller (5)
17 Jewish priest (5)
18 Rare gas (4)
22 Arabian gazelle (5)
23 Free time (7)
24 Informal (6)
25 Purpose (6)

Down

1 Self-opinionated types (7)
2 Shakespearean play (7)
3 Map (5)
4 Tight group (7)
5 Mexican Indian (5)
6 German steel town (5)
9 Veto election to club (9)
14 Dramatic scene (7)
15 Formal gift (7)
16 Aerial (7)
19 Timepiece (5)
20 Slightly drunk (5)
21 Mean person (5)

Across

1 Salvers (5)
4 Beach (5)
10 Young child (7)
11 Writer of fables (5)
12 Breed of dog (5)
13 Astonish (7)
15 Bird's home (4)
17 Saturated (5)
19 Apart (5)
22 Monster (4)
25 Train (7)
27 Enumerate (5)
29 Upright (5)
30 Get-together (7)
31 Look hard (5)
32 Diary-writer (5)

Down

2 Horseman (5)
3 Shouting (7)
5 Centre (5)
6 Saved (7)
7 Adhere (5)
8 Regions (5)
9 Gardening tool (5)
14 Heavenly body (4)
16 Island (4)
18 Rich (7)
20 Hide (7)
21 Gem (5)
23 Bacilli (5)
24 Platform (5)
26 Performer (5)
28 Oneness (5)

62

Across

1 One who scorns (6)
4 Tableaux (6)
7 Catapult (9)
9 Voice register (4)
10 Filter (4)
11 Drink (5)
13 *Arabian Nights* hero (6)
14 Contemporary (6)
15 Alloy (6)
17 Herb (6)
19 River of Italy (5)
20 Canned herring (4)
22 Continent (4)
23 Arduous (9)
24 Depart (3,3)
25 Slip by (6)

Down

1 Swamp (6)
2 Unit of mass (4)
3 Putrid (6)
4 Method (6)
5 God of love (4)
6 Muslim ruler (6)
7 Play defensive cricket (9)
8 Fatigue (9)
11 Military pupil (5)
12 Wanderer (5)
15 Sign of the Zodiac (6)
16 Financial exploitation (3-3)
17 Catlike (6)
18 Alliance (6)
21 Skirting-board (4)
22 Atmosphere (4)

Across

1 Puncturing (8)
7 Cetacean mammal (5)
8 Work together (2-7)
9 Marriage portion (3)
10 Speaking platform (4)
11 Campanile (6)
13 Roman emperor (6)
14 Cowardly (6)
17 Sternly (6)
18 Unruly child (4)
20 In addition (3)
22 Hero-worship (9)
23 Take it easy (5)
24 Contemptible (8)

Down

1 Walked up and down (5)
2 Wearing away (7)
3 Professional cook (4)
4 Closer (6)
5 Lewd (5)
6 Have reference to (7)
7 General prosperity (7)
12 Nova Scotian capital (7)
13 Water-tank (7)
15 Giddiness (7)
16 Entice (6)
17 Devout (5)
19 Pungent (5)
21 Indian dress (4)

64

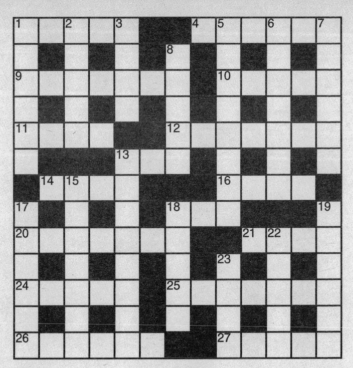

Across

1 Northern Ireland city (5)
4 Lapped (6)
9 Swaggering talk (7)
10 Tendon (5)
11 Greek letter (4)
12 Amusing (7)
13 Tree (3)
14 Fall (4)
16 Guessing game (1-3)
18 Pasture (3)
20 Sturgeon's roe (7)
21 Blemish (4)
24 Snow leopard (5)
25 Reptile (7)
26 Score (6)
27 Premature (5)

Down

1 Rubbish (6)
2 Banter (5)
3 Period of time (4)
5 Sleeplessness (8)
6 Marsh-marigold (7)
7 Loiter (6)
8 Trainer (5)
13 Obvious (8)
15 Income (7)
17 Confront (6)
18 Minimum (5)
19 Attractive (6)
22 Transparent (5)
23 Cheese (4)

Across

1 Numerical chart (5)
4 Packet covering (7)
8 Puzzle (7)
9 Heavy rain (5)
10 Stop-watch (5)
11 Continent (7)
13 Entrance (4)
15 Ill clad (6)
17 Murderer (6)
20 Simple (4)
22 Clothing (7)
24 Complete overhaul (5)
26 Freshwater fish (5)
27 Keep out (7)
28 Swindled (7)
29 Illumination (5)

Down

1 Betting adviser (7)
2 Sweeping implement (5)
3 Make bigger (7)
4 Australian marsupial (6)
5 Passage through church (5)
6 Honesty (7)
7 Cuban dance (5)
12 Disorder (4)
14 Eastern port (4)
16 Necklace of flowers (7)
18 Poetic (7)
19 Draw back (7)
21 Wait upon (6)
22 Injured by bull (5)
23 An alcohol (5)
25 Threw (5)

66

Across

1 Island near Tenby (6)
4 Dismisses (5)
8 Sense (5)
9 Colleague (7)
10 Word for word (7)
11 Wear away (4)
12 Fall behind (3)
14 District (4)
15 Speed contest (4)
18 Limb (3)
21 Impel (4)
23 Scottish region (7)
25 Grasshopper (7)
26 Religious ascetic (5)
27 French sculptor (5)
28 Cheerful (6)

Down

1 Fortress (6)
2 Boat (7)
3 Outside (8)
4 Foam (4)
5 Ecclesiastical rule (5)
6 Spread out (6)
7 Overturn (5)
13 Thankful (8)
16 Insect (7)
17 Friend (6)
19 Move smoothly (5)
20 Incorrect (6)
22 Confined to college (5)
24 Cumbrian river (4)

Across

1 Colour-changers (5)
4 Characteristics (6)
9 Type of dog (7)
10 Commerce (5)
11 Scold (4)
12 Fortune-teller (7)
13 Hatchet (3)
14 Unseal (4)
16 Stalk (4)
18 Donkey (3)
20 Cautious (7)
21 Despondent (4)
24 Correct (5)
25 Shorten (7)
26 Bear (6)
27 Prodigious (5)

Down

1 Want (6)
2 Precise (5)
3 Slender (4)
5 Merciless (8)
6 Envision (7)
7 Detective (6)
8 Incline (5)
13 Forebear (8)
15 Stoppered (7)
17 Meagre (6)
18 Map-collection (5)
19 Flaw (6)
22 Shelf (5)
23 Boast (4)

68

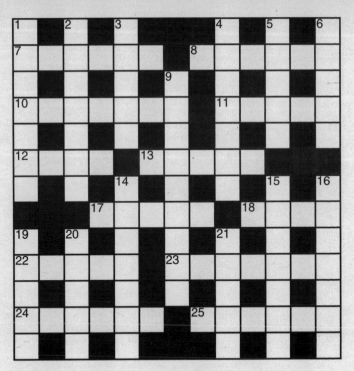

Across

7 Confederation (6)
8 Collaborators (6)
10 Gnomon (7)
11 Collier (5)
12 Simple (4)
13 Convent (5)
17 Tempest (5)
18 Over and done with (4)
22 Fish (5)
23 Acrobat (7)
24 Occupier (6)
25 Furrow (6)

Down

1 Confuse (7)
2 Shellac (7)
3 Gruesome (5)
4 Climb awkwardly (7)
5 Demon (5)
6 Commandeer (5)
9 Detailed (9)
14 Staying-power (7)
15 French-speaking
   Belgium (7)
16 Racing official (7)
19 Die down (5)
20 Mock assault (5)
21 Silly smile (5)

Across

1 Navigates (5)
4 Cheap buy (7)
8 Disordered (7)
9 Puzzle (5)
10 Blood-sucking worm (5)
11 Arbitrate (7)
13 Pitcher (4)
15 Mob (6)
17 Spiritualistic session (6)
20 Holly (4)
22 Wine-jar (7)
24 Factory (5)
26 Significance (5)
27 Shift (7)
28 Fan (7)
29 Exhausted (5)

Down

1 Worldly (7)
2 Statue (5)
3 School bag (7)
4 Suited (6)
5 Speedy (5)
6 Decline to vote (7)
7 Audacity (5)
12 Gaelic (4)
14 Low dam (4)
16 Christian sacrament (7)
18 Non-stop train (7)
19 Beseech (7)
21 Cavalryman (6)
22 Greek 'a' (5)
23 Farther from centre (5)
25 Nimble (5)

70

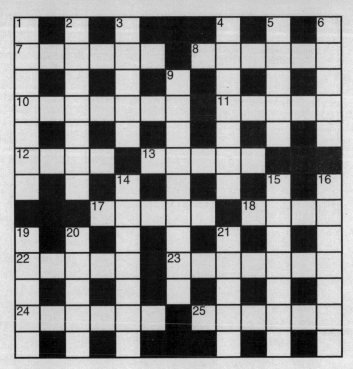

Across

7 Aircraft (6)
8 In poor health (6)
10 Wind instrument (7)
11 Insect (5)
12 Frolic (4)
13 Nursemaid (5)
17 Monk (5)
18 Lake (4)
22 Overweight (5)
23 Imitate (7)
24 Rat (6)
25 Small restaurant (6)

Down

1 Flat spoon (7)
2 Month (7)
3 Entice (5)
4 Precious stone (7)
5 Light-headed (5)
6 Consent (5)
9 Tactic (9)
14 Gift (7)
15 Fine (7)
16 Mature (7)
19 Trouble (sl.) (5)
20 Verbose (5)
21 Roman god (5)

Across

1 Crave after (6)
4 Tribal leaders (6)
7 Threaten with exposure (9)
9 Aquatic mammal (4)
10 Certain (4)
11 Horizontal (5)
13 System (6)
14 Memorised (6)
15 Death (6)
17 Tropic (6)
19 Mistake (5)
20 Author of Utopia (4)
22 Wound with dagger (4)
23 Get rid of entirely (9)
24 Rely (6)
25 French painter (6)

Down

1 Horse-drawn cab (6)
2 Murder (4)
3 Moved to and fro (6)
4 Force (6)
5 Pigmented area of eye (4)
6 Noiseless (6)
7 Maryland city (9)
8 Oil or grease (9)
11 Vermin (5)
12 Hungarian opera writer (5)
15 Forcibly require (6)
16 Worn away (6)
17 Agree (6)
18 Thief (6)
21 Gaelic (4)
22 Knock unconscious (4)

72

Across

1 The Eternal City (4)
3 Old relics (8)
9 Adder (5)
10 Huge (7)
11 Fabulous bird (3)
13 Outer edge (9)
14 Dilapidated old car (6)
16 Egyptian god (6)
18 Polite (9)
20 Illuminated (3)
22 Bloodlessness (7)
23 Thread (5)
25 Drew (8)
26 Go out (4)

Down

1 Wanderer (5)
2 Plan (3)
4 Innate character (6)
5 Narrow neck of land (7)
6 Abnormal (9)
7 Makes safe (7)
8 Hold (4)
12 Work out (9)
14 Stupid person (7)
15 US river (7)
17 Search for food (6)
19 Couch (4)
21 Handle (5)
24 Evergreen shrub (3)

Across

1 Destroyed (7)
5 Musical work (5)
8 Sung drama (5)
9 Wash (7)
10 Beg (7)
11 Concur (5)
12 Package (6)
14 Leave (6)
17 Chart (5)
19 Instance (7)
22 Aslope (7)
23 Pungent (5)
24 Amid (5)
25 Determine (7)

Down

1 Inscribed (5)
2 Voter (7)
3 Rogue (5)
4 Expunge (6)
5 Train (7)
6 Beneath (5)
7 Serious (7)
12 Kneecap (7)
13 Late-day (7)
15 Clothing (7)
16 Mendicant (6)
18 Jollification (5)
20 Gather together (5)
21 Supply (5)

Across

1 More serene (6)
4 Sets fire to (6)
7 Obedient (9)
9 Fat (4)
10 Grasp (4)
11 Avarice (5)
13 Small gate (6)
14 Harrier (6)
15 Mend (6)
17 Roman general (6)
19 Uncanny (5)
20 Wagers (4)
22 Heraldic devices (4)
23 Sleepy (9)
24 Flowing (6)
25 Jeopardy (6)

Down

1 Immature (6)
2 Frame of mind (4)
3 Explosion (6)
4 Dawdle (6)
5 Percussion instrument (4)
6 Daze (6)
7 Crazy persons (9)
8 Captivate (9)
11 Arabian demon (5)
12 Blockhead (5)
15 Snub (6)
16 Milk-curdling substance (6)
17 Sneaked (6)
18 Shellfish (6)
21 Flat fish (4)
22 Presently (4)

Across

1 Leader of the House (4)
3 Weird (8)
9 Brush (5)
10 Appendix to will (7)
11 Sweet potato (3)
13 Rising again (9)
14 Passion (6)
16 Fictional works (6)
18 Examination by questions (9)
20 Gratuity (3)
22 Going firm (7)
23 Private teacher (5)
25 Mentally unbalanced (8)
26 Disavow (4)

Down

1 Pastime (5)
2 Court (3)
4 Superfluity (6)
5 Endure (7)
6 Merciless (9)
7 Recounts (7)
8 Muslim ruler (4)
12 Reflective person (9)
14 Charged (7)
15 Anointing with oil (7)
17 Unmarried (6)
19 Small arachnid (4)
21 Ward off (5)
24 Draw (3)

76

Across

1 View (7)
5 European race (5)
8 Mix (5)
9 Go forward (7)
10 Drudgery (7)
11 Watering place (5)
12 Paying guest (6)
14 Dark red (6)
17 Apple wine (5)
19 Betrayer (7)
22 Light dressing-gown (7)
23 Evidence (5)
24 Provide (5)
25 Glisten (7)

Down

1 Circuitous path (5)
2 N. Atlantic republic (7)
3 Subcontinent (5)
4 Almost (6)
5 Russian ballerina (7)
6 Yearns (5)
7 Large hat (7)
12 Terse (7)
13 Before now (7)
15 Prospect (7)
16 Emphasise (6)
18 Number (5)
20 Greek letter (5)
21 Firearm (5)

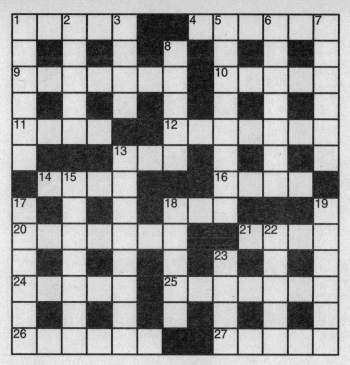

Across

1 One who accepts a bet (5)
4 Goose cock (6)
9 Journeyed overland (7)
10 Criminally assaulted (5)
11 Conceal (4)
12 Winged horse (7)
13 Humour (3)
14 The maple (4)
16 Neat (4)
18 Recline (3)
20 Concentrated (7)
21 Volcanic outflow (4)
24 Pertaining to hearing (5)
25 Conspirator (7)
26 Way out (6)
27 A burgundy wine (5)

Down

1 Irritable (6)
2 Work dough (5)
3 Improvident type (4)
5 Claim without right (8)
6 Removed from high position (7)
7 Root vegetable (6)
8 Skilled (5)
13 Creases (8)
15 Provider of food (7)
17 Storm of abuse (6)
18 Jumped (5)
19 Fruitless (6)
22 Frolic (5)
23 Destiny (4)

78

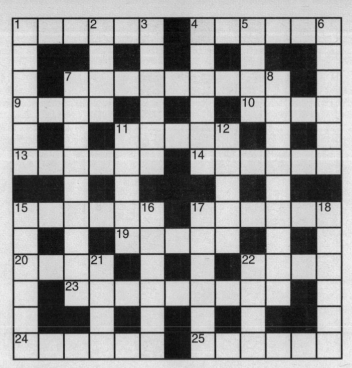

Across

1 Sheep's flesh (6)
4 Scottish magistrate (6)
7 Bizarre (9)
9 Funeral pile (4)
10 Body of the church (4)
11 Be of service (5)
13 Prairie-wolf (6)
14 Messenger (6)
15 Forceless (6)
17 Complete failure (6)
19 Swollen (5)
20 Poet (4)
22 Flog (4)
23 Guide (9)
24 Dome (6)
25 Stay behind (6)

Down

1 Short-sighted (6)
2 Rubber tube (4)
3 Inherent (6)
4 Arouse (6)
5 Spanish border town (4)
6 Captivate (6)
7 Old man (9)
8 Seriously (9)
11 Leaning (5)
12 Ghastly (5)
15 Structure (6)
16 Exclamation of triumph (6)
17 Percolate (6)
18 Gas (6)
21 Queen of Carthage (4)
22 Away (4)

Across

7 Confederation (6)
8 Helpers (6)
10 Monk's haircut (7)
11 Dodge (5)
12 Above (4)
13 Shore (5)
17 Bet (5)
18 Avid (4)
22 Watchful (5)
23 Cut short (7)
24 Try hard (6)
25 Grotto (6)

Down

1 Euphoria (7)
2 Artist (7)
3 Dawn (3-2)
4 Eloquence (7)
5 Bed (5)
6 Willow (5)
9 Mention (9)
14 Prisoner (7)
15 Akin (7)
16 Lean (7)
19 Lift (5)
20 Centre (5)
21 Smash (5)

80

Across

1 Photographs (6)
4 Part of flower (5)
8 Crest (5)
9 EEC member (7)
10 Marsupial (7)
11 Large book (4)
12 Young flower (3)
14 Russian emperor (4)
15 Rim (4)
18 Terminate (3)
21 Male voice (4)
23 Hanging about (7)
25 Table game (7)
26 Gemstone (5)
27 Tax (5)
28 Protect (6)

Down

1 Forgive (6)
2 At home (7)
3 Riches (8)
4 Fabric (4)
5 Greek philosopher (5)
6 Steps (6)
7 Digit (5)
13 Fragile (8)
16 Ugly expression (7)
17 Hound (6)
19 Undersized person (5)
20 Consented (6)
22 Fish (5)
24 Scottish isle (4)

Across

1 Let (7)
5 Din (5)
8 Supple (5)
9 On the sheltered side (7)
10 Place of refuge (9)
12 Atmospheric condensation (3)
13 Procession (6)
14 Restrained (6)
17 Pastry dish (3)
18 Intrepid (9)
20 Inauspicious (7)
21 Parent's brother (5)
23 Listlessness (5)
24 Breathed in (7)

Down

1 Book of maps (5)
2 Illuminated (3)
3 Sharpened (7)
4 Texan city (6)
5 Indigent (5)
6 Impossible to hear (9)
7 Bequeathed income to (7)
11 Scandinavian (9)
13 Red Indian baby (7)
15 Lie (7)
16 Breakfast cereal (6)
18 Loincloth (5)
19 Velocity (5)
22 Mountain pass (3)

Across

1 Perused (4)
3 Streams (8)
9 Clergyman (5)
10 Whole number (7)
11 Auction item (3)
13 Complained (9)
14 Wither (6)
16 Wanders (6)
18 Strive (9)
20 Tree (3)
22 Time of day (7)
23 Amusing (5)
25 Outfit (8)
26 Sketch (4)

Down

1 Opponent (5)
2 Curve (3)
4 Complete agreement (6)
5 Withdrawal (7)
6 Frightening vision (9)
7 Steps out (7)
8 Journey (4)
12 Residents (anag) (9)
14 Go before (7)
15 Sports ground (7)
17 Asiatic language (6)
19 Affluent (4)
21 Parrot (5)
24 Spoil (3)

Across

1 Bower (6)
4 Original stencil (6)
7 Logic (9)
9 Lord Avon (4)
10 Unfailingly loyal (4)
11 Loose hairnet (5)
13 Executed quickly (6)
14 Feel remorse (6)
15 Decorous (6)
17 Shoved (6)
19 Social distinction (5)
20 Pakistani province (4)
22 Without charge (4)
23 Duplicity (9)
24 Treeless Arctic region (6)
25 Shrieked (6)

Down

1 Dormant (6)
2 Portent (4)
3 Take umbrage at (6)
4 Trusted adviser (6)
5 Dispatched (4)
6 Discard (6)
7 Counsel (9)
8 Rookie (9)
11 Lean (5)
12 First public appearance (5)
15 Cease (6)
16 Skin inflammation (6)
17 Larder (6)
18 Judged (6)
21 Lifeless (4)
22 Young horse (4)

Across

1 System of belief (5)
4 Take place (5)
10 Skittle (7)
11 Respond (5)
12 Engulf (5)
13 Evicted (7)
15 Certain (4)
17 Frequently (5)
19 —— Island Red (5)
22 Nobleman (4)
25 Card game (7)
27 Recapitulate (3,2)
29 Separately (5)
30 Stupid (7)
31 Condemn (5)
32 Oneness (5)

Down

2 Musical composition (5)
3 Outlay (7)
5 Slice (5)
6 Not performed (7)
7 Slyly derogatory (5)
8 Enrage (5)
9 Scrutinise (5)
14 Sudden movement (4)
16 Unfasten (4)
18 Flourish of trumpets (7)
20 Sackcloth (7)
21 Small fish (5)
23 Unsuitable (5)
24 Condiment (5)
26 Aquatic mammal (5)
28 Anthem (5)

Across

1 Middle (6)
4 Talons (5)
8 Consumed (5)
9 Inflexible (7)
10 Gravel (7)
11 Rim (4)
12 Decay (3)
14 Old (4)
15 Italian capital (4)
18 Age (3)
21 Badgers' burrow (4)
23 Pupil (7)
25 Ugly sight (7)
26 Male relative (5)
27 Instructor (5)
28 Arid area (6)

Down

1 Fold (6)
2 Nil (7)
3 Traitor (8)
4 Crustacean (4)
5 Prize (5)
6 Sofa (6)
7 Vacillate (5)
13 Value (8)
16 Fetter (7)
17 Agree (6)
19 Foreigner (5)
20 Keen (6)
22 Robbery (5)
24 Indigent (4)

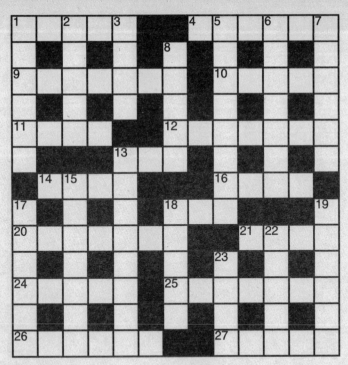

Across

1 A relish (5)
4 Mistakes (6)
9 Chorus (7)
10 Come in (5)
11 Electricity unit (4)
12 Cuisine (7)
13 Tree (3)
14 Flaccid (4)
16 On strike (4)
18 Curve (3)
20 Agreement (7)
21 Highest point (4)
24 Lassitude (5)
25 Fast train (7)
26 Sampled (6)
27 German city (5)

Down

1 Canny (6)
2 Ailing (5)
3 Kind of cheese (4)
5 Oratory (8)
6 Porridge (7)
7 Wanders (6)
8 Light meal (5)
13 Converse (8)
15 Batting team (7)
17 Receive (6)
18 Viper (5)
19 Learning period (6)
22 Board game (5)
23 Fencing sword (4)

Across

1 Fireplace (5)
4 Antarctic explorer (5)
10 Iraqi capital (7)
11 Mountain chain (5)
12 Incantation (5)
13 Four-sided figure (7)
15 Sea eagle (4)
17 Paris underground (5)
19 Shiny black (5)
22 Before long (4)
25 Pulverised (7)
27 Characteristic (5)
29 Narcotic drug (5)
30 Impious (7)
31 African grassland (5)
32 Unquestioning belief (5)

Down

2 Scoundrel (5)
3 Tiny fish (7)
5 Freight (5)
6 Defensible (7)
7 Humiliate (5)
8 Festoon (5)
9 Thong (5)
14 Leading man (4)
16 Rebelled (4)
18 Learned (7)
20 West Indian island (7)
21 Journalistic coup (5)
23 Hatred (5)
24 Corset (5)
26 Moist (5)
28 Accounts inspection (5)

88

Across

7 Violent outcry (6)
8 Looks intently (6)
10 Chinese panacea (7)
11 Surpass (5)
12 Wild goat (4)
13 Parsonage (5)
17 Merriment (5)
18 Roman censor (4)
22 Lengthwise (5)
23 Retribution (7)
24 Homily (6)
25 Attractiveness (6)

Down

1 Lady's maid (7)
2 Slim (7)
3 Nectar (5)
4 Disbeliever (7)
5 Cocaine product (5)
6 Sacred song (5)
9 Inelegant (anag.) (9)
14 Realm (7)
15 Faint (4,3)
16 A brief (7)
19 Out-of-date (5)
20 Woo (5)
21 Diminutive (5)

Across

1 Gloomy (4)
3 Bird (8)
9 English poet (5)
10 Dwelt (7)
11 Society girl (3)
13 Sorrow (9)
14 Slang (6)
16 Joked (6)
18 Inkling (9)
20 Strike (3)
22 Poorer (7)
23 Imprecise (5)
25 Wilted (8)
26 Kind (4)

Down

1 Decay (2,3)
2 Sin (3)
4 Menace (6)
5 Ornament of ribbons (7)
6 Pointer (9)
7 Something particularly timely (3-4)
8 Move slowly (4)
12 Chinese soup (5-4)
14 Short time ago (4,3)
15 Opening (7)
17 Savage (6)
19 Star (4)
21 Bit (5)
24 Steadying rope (3)

90

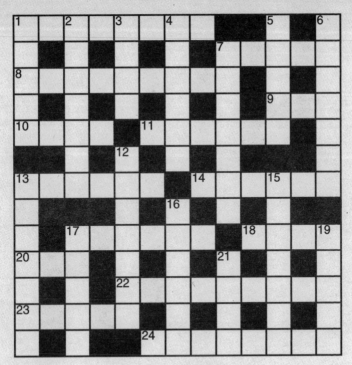

Across

1 Ignore (8)
7 Shelters (5)
8 Dismal-looking (9)
9 Spirit (3)
10 Twelve months (4)
11 Bustle (6)
13 Puzzle (6)
14 Document (6)
17 Marshy (6)
18 Machine-gun (4)
20 Circuit (3)
22 Partner (9)
23 Steam bath (5)
24 Carry on (8)

Down

1 Marriage portion (5)
2 Whole affair (7)
3 Comply (4)
4 Blockhead (6)
5 Cross (5)
6 Son of Abraham (7)
7 Row of houses (7)
12 W Indian island (7)
13 Unemployed (7)
15 Eight-sided figure (7)
16 US spacecraft (6)
17 Jet (5)
19 Relative (5)
21 Undergarment (4)

Across

1 Smell (5)
4 Replica (5)
10 Put down (7)
11 Flexible (5)
12 Additional (5)
13 Attribute (7)
15 Repose (4)
17 Scene (5)
19 Greek letter (5)
22 Mature (4)
25 Lost (7)
27 Separate (5)
29 Perfume (5)
30 Neat (7)
31 Tempest (5)
32 Strove (5)

Down

2 Storehouse (5)
3 Parvenu (7)
5 Garden shrub (5)
6 Nil (7)
7 Layabout (5)
8 Book of maps (5)
9 Flat (5)
14 Cease (4)
16 Merit (4)
18 Examine (7)
20 Wind about (7)
21 Collect (5)
23 Snow-house (5)
24 Remains (5)
26 Bury (5)
28 Eagle's nest (5)

Across

1 Precious stone (5)
4 Aim (7)
8 Wife of Ahab (7)
9 Small group (5)
10 Male voice (5)
11 Swarm (7)
13 US state (4)
15 Disburden (6)
17 Recollection (6)
20 Detect (4)
22 Gain (7)
24 Moral principle (5)
26 Piping (5)
27 Restrain (7)
28 Songster (7)
29 Audacious attempt (3-2)

Down

1 Judo (2-5)
2 Dried up (5)
3 African country (7)
4 Cushion (6)
5 European river (5)
6 Canadian province (7)
7 Swallowed (5)
12 Patch up (4)
14 European river (4)
16 Alcoholic drink (7)
18 Range of vision (7)
19 Mexican peninsula (7)
21 Elder (6)
22 Weapon (5)
23 Poem (5)
25 Pastime (5)

Across

1 Elapsed (6)
4 Taut (5)
8 Muscular contraction (5)
9 Bitterness (7)
10 Idiotic (7)
11 Dregs (4)
12 Essay (3)
14 Military cap (4)
15 Detect (4)
18 Reverence (3)
21 European mountains (4)
23 Virulent satire (7)
25 Sluggish (7)
26 Lowest point (5)
27 Hidden store (5)
28 Of mixed ancestry (6)

Down

1 Calm (6)
2 Take by surprise (7)
3 Jubilation (8)
4 Minute (4)
5 Lasso (5)
6 Way out (6)
7 Believe in (5)
13 Class of freeholders (8)
16 More haughty (7)
17 French (6)
19 Cunningly avoid (5)
20 Trapped (6)
22 Carthaginian (5)
24 Unsullied (4)

Across

1 Wharf (4)
3 Set in place (8)
9 Overweight (5)
10 Appliances (7)
11 Beast of burden (3)
13 Veronica (9)
14 Punctual (6)
16 Comrade (6)
18 Place of worship (9)
20 Add up (3)
22 Stunning (7)
23 Frequently (5)
25 Fabulous country (2,6)
26 Powder (4)

Down

1 Share (5)
2 Imitate (3)
4 Abundance (6)
5 Aggressor (7)
6 Stormy (9)
7 Cuddled up (7)
8 Liquor sediment (4)
12 Dash north (anag) (9)
14 Mattock (7)
15 First minister (7)
17 Cold (6)
19 Weaving machine (4)
21 Pick-me-up (5)
24 Beverage (3)

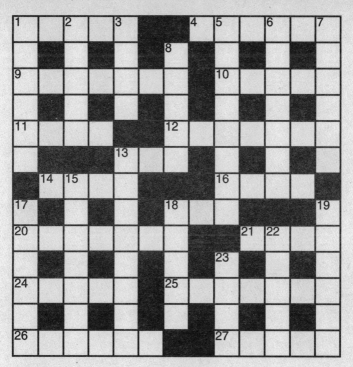

Across

1 Totally open (5)
4 Worked for money (6)
9 Unimportant (7)
10 Canal boat (5)
11 Given to modern culture (4)
12 Unimaginatively expressed (7)
13 Pastry dish (3)
14 Agitate (4)
16 Thing (4)
18 Brewed beverage (3)
20 Tutor (7)
21 Hebridean isle (4)
24 Morsel of bread (5)
25 Root vegetable (7)
26 Detective (6)
27 Russian aristocrat (5)

Down

1 Criminal (6)
2 Promulgation (5)
3 Labour (4)
5 Food of the gods (8)
6 Tell (7)
7 Wet thoroughly (6)
8 Incline (5)
13 Ban (8)
15 Speak maliciously (7)
17 Reserves (6)
18 Meat from stomach (5)
19 Guard (6)
22 Of deviant character (5)
23 Seize (4)

Across

1 Banner (8)
7 Cake covering (5)
8 Traveller (9)
9 Bird (3)
10 Gloomy (4)
11 Stringed instrument (6)
13 Autonomous board (6)
14 Brisk (6)
17 Stitch (6)
18 Musical symbol (4)
20 Carve (3)
22 Nitre (9)
23 Temporary doctor (5)
24 Clearly stated (8)

Down

1 Tasty (5)
2 European country (7)
3 Intense (4)
4 Recover (6)
5 Wild ox (5)
6 Nimbleness (7)
7 Eire (7)
12 Self-conceit (7)
13 Rapidly (7)
15 Prudent (7)
16 Long-winded (6)
17 Pile of hay (5)
19 Navy (5)
21 Gemstone (4)

Across

1 Peal (5)
4 German capital (6)
9 Pharmacist (7)
10 Zest (5)
11 Brook (4)
12 Perfume (7)
13 Request (3)
14 Region (4)
16 Require (4)
18 Perform (3)
20 Hampered (7)
21 Short letter (4)
24 Dutch cheese (5)
25 Complain (7)
26 Utters (6)
27 Male singer (5)

Down

1 Roman writer (6)
2 Perfect (5)
3 Egress (4)
5 Aubergine (8)
6 Pasta dish (7)
7 Halters (6)
8 Adhere (5)
13 Anteater (8)
15 Ecstasy (7)
17 Burns (6)
18 Accomplished (5)
19 Superior (6)
22 Sea (5)
23 Footwear (4)

98

Across

1 Clergyman (6)
4 Raise anchor (5)
8 Italian city (5)
9 Huge statues (7)
10 Most favourable (7)
11 Tare (4)
12 Young animal (3)
14 So let it be (4)
15 Discourteous (4)
18 Light knock (3)
21 American tramp (4)
23 Thing added (7)
25 Laughable (7)
26 Stunned (5)
27 Inconsiderate speed (5)
28 Shed (4-2)

Down

1 Snake (6)
2 Layer (7)
3 Decoration (8)
4 Testament (4)
5 Offspring (5)
6 Coiffure (4-2)
7 Rogue (5)
13 Condemn unheard (8)
16 Inhabitant (7)
17 Place of worship (6)
19 Communion plate (5)
20 Workroom (6)
22 Foundation (5)
24 French priest (4)

Across

5 Candid (5)
8 Famous physicist (8)
9 Open-mouthed (5)
10 Execution platform (8)
11 Bulgarian capital (5)
14 Choose (3)
16 Euphoric (6)
17 By word of mouth (6)
18 Slope downwards (3)
20 Monastic superior (5)
24 Not genuine (8)
25 Lawful (5)
26 Antiquarian guide (8)
27 Unexpected obstacles (5)

Down

1 Card (5)
2 School telltale (5)
3 Inflexible (5)
4 Stimulus (6)
6 Local (8)
7 Wedding ceremony (8)
12 Vulgar (8)
13 Bending over (8)
14 Weird (3)
15 Spinning toy (3)
19 Damage (6)
21 Thin porridge (5)
22 Punctuation-mark (5)
23 Awry (5)

Across

7 Young swan (6)
8 Ruminant (6)
10 Miserable (7)
11 Topic (5)
12 Fabricator (4)
13 Mode of expression (5)
17 Tranquillity (5)
18 Fairy (4)
22 Tax (5)
23 Fabric (7)
24 EEC member (6)
25 Yell (6)

Down

1 Small weight (7)
2 Intellectual (7)
3 Lure (5)
4 Nondescript article (7)
5 Sugary (5)
6 Wept (5)
9 Combine (9)
14 Du Maurier titular heroine (7)
15 Unit of sound (7)
16 Quandary (7)
19 Personnel (5)
20 Wander (5)
21 Precise (5)

Across

1 European language (6)
4 Another European language (6)
7 Gaiety (9)
9 Spoke falsely (4)
10 Amused expression (4)
11 Highland instrumentalist (5)
13 French scientist (6)
14 Skin (6)
15 Cold (6)
17 Roar like a bull (6)
19 A ductile element (5)
20 Solicit business (4)
22 Invisible emanation (4)
23 Immodest (9)
24 Decayed (6)
25 Gland below thyroid (6)

Down

1 Boost (6)
2 Require (4)
3 Recluse (6)
4 Inflated (6)
5 Breathing organ (4)
6 Places regularly frequented (6)
7 Musically pleasant (9)
8 Shaking (9)
11 Davidic hymn (5)
12 Insurgent (5)
15 Fast sailing ship (6)
16 Small freeholder (6)
17 Vote (6)
18 Marine animals (6)
21 The item indicated (4)
22 Grey (4)

102

Across

1 Hickory nut (5)
4 Masticates (5)
10 Rhyme (7)
11 Rectangular block (5)
12 Papaya (5)
13 Quick rapping sound (3-1-3)
15 Sea-eagle (4)
17 Slip (5)
19 Tender (5)
22 Not any (4)
25 Satire (7)
27 Jewish leader (5)
29 Keep short (5)
30 Pressing (7)
31 Open-mouthed (5)
32 More modern (5)

Down

2 Furnish (5)
3 Admitted (7)
5 Custom (5)
6 High-pitched sound (7)
7 Picture of scenery (5)
8 Strict (5)
9 Kind of ray (5)
14 Vast age (4)
16 US divorce city (4)
18 Rodent (7)
20 Productive (7)
21 Fastening (5)
23 Start (5)
24 Same again (5)
26 Winning (2,3)
28 Musical note (5)

Across

1 Areas (7)
5 Doctor (5)
8 Strength (5)
9 German city (7)
10 Got together (9)
12 Tune (3)
13 Puissant (6)
14 Improve (6)
17 And so on (3)
18 Indoor game (9)
20 Worship (7)
21 Normal (5)
23 Discrimination (5)
24 Vista (7)

Down

1 Cuban dance (5)
2 Joke (3)
3 Turkish (7)
4 Rider's seat (6)
5 Walk (5)
6 Attempt (9)
7 Fit of temper (7)
11 Wise (9)
13 Pharmacist (7)
15 Gastronome (7)
16 Foreigners (6)
18 Salt-water (5)
19 Stupid (5)
22 Employ (3)

104

Across

1 Shrub with red berries (5)
4 Absconds (7)
8 Love affair (7)
9 Month (5)
10 Broom (5)
11 Oriental (7)
13 Ventilates (4)
15 Underpants (6)
17 Wife of Tristan (6)
20 Advance (4)
22 Porcelain town (7)
24 Spirits dispenser (5)
26 Sailing-vessel (5)
27 Gauche (7)
28 Behest (7)
29 Measuring strip (5)

Down

1 Fish (7)
2 Consignments (5)
3 Face-veil (7)
4 Jeopardy (6)
5 Bedlam (5)
6 Eng. poet (7)
7 Hairdresser's premises (5)
12 Continent (4)
14 Lies (anag) (4)
16 Regular (7)
18 Thwart (7)
19 One who uses ciphers (7)
21 Toward position ahead (6)
22 Harmony (5)
23 Brown pigment (5)
25 Straggle (5)

Across

1 Clairvaux saint (7)
5 Coast (5)
8 Requirements (5)
9 Water-bearing rock (7)
10 Eulogistic (9)
12 Pony (3)
13 Show off (6)
14 Imitated (6)
17 Python (3)
18 Intrepid (9)
20 Mortified (7)
21 Musical works (5)
23 Phoenician city (5)
24 Corrected (7)

Down

1 Commonplace (5)
2 Feel remorse (3)
3 Be teetotal (7)
4 Minor cleric (6)
5 Impudent (5)
6 Military initiative (9)
7 Infuriated (7)
11 Not discomfited (9)
13 Socialist associates (7)
15 Result (7)
16 Gautama Siddhartha (6)
18 Evil spirit (5)
19 Pottery fragment (5)
22 Conclusion (3)

106

Across

1 Arab prince (6)
4 Pointed weapon (5)
8 Trim feathers (5)
9 VAT exemption (3-4)
10 Set apart (7)
11 French cheese (4)
12 Indistinct (3)
14 Withhold assent (4)
15 Original sinner (4)
18 Peculiar (3)
21 Friend (4)
23 Show delight (7)
25 Wednesday (7)
26 Aristocratic (5)
27 Staggers (5)
28 Consented (6)

Down

1 Girl's name (6)
2 Offensive blemish (7)
3 Marsupial (8)
4 Colour (4)
5 Mistake (5)
6 Jacket (6)
7 Horse (5)
13 Chinese game (3-5)
16 Pheasant (7)
17 Land worker (6)
19 Male duck (5)
20 Rely on (6)
22 Shelf (5)
24 Wagers (4)

Across

7 West country river (6)
8 Rowing teams (6)
10 Brave woman (7)
11 Face cosmetic (5)
12 Burglar's swag (4)
13 Large box (5)
17 Wander aimlessly (5)
18 Be irritated (4)
22 Pursue (5)
23 Sincere (7)
24 In truth (6)
25 High-level computer language (6)

Down

1 Bitumenous surface (7)
2 Football team (7)
3 Characteristic (5)
4 Move to foreign parts (7)
5 Call loudly (5)
6 Flower (5)
9 Very frightened (9)
14 Tidy (7)
15 Extend (7)
16 Space craft (7)
19 Oak seed (5)
20 Trite (5)
21 Keyboard instrument (5)

Across

1 Cold and damp (6)
4 Country (6)
7 Astrologer (4-5)
9 Fixing agent (4)
10 Thaw (4)
11 Doctrine (5)
13 Cad (6)
14 Twofold (6)
15 Twinge (6)
17 Straightforward (6)
19 Discover (3,2)
20 Dull pain (4)
22 Continent (4)
23 Closely integrated (5-4)
24 Become visible (6)
25 In fact (6)

Down

1 Somewhat (6)
2 Until (2,2)
3 Cricket ball (6)
4 Approached (6)
5 Pour (4)
6 Irritate (6)
7 Focus of attention (9)
8 Robin (9)
11 Instruct (5)
12 Poison (5)
15 Emotional shock (6)
16 To this place (6)
17 Stevedore (6)
18 Worthless (6)
21 Republic of Ireland (4)
22 Verdi opera (4)

109

Across

1 Scattered rubbish (6)
4 Octet (5)
8 Rips (5)
9 Chic (7)
10 Train (7)
11 Inactive (4)
12 Cereal (3)
14 Abominable snowman (4)
15 Requirement (4)
18 Tin (3)
21 Tale (4)
23 Late (7)
25 Wearisome (7)
26 Cap (5)
27 Wash (5)
28 Hard (6)

Down

1 Missive (6)
2 Calumniate (7)
3 Euphoric (8)
4 Sheep (4)
5 Impressive (5)
6 Leash (6)
7 At no time (5)
13 Outfit (8)
16 Recommend (7)
17 Shellfish (6)
19 Din (5)
20 Insect (6)
22 French sculptor (5)
24 Manage (4)

110

Across

1 Not treated with spade (5)
4 Essex port (7)
8 Freakish (7)
9 City of India (5)
10 Cancel (5)
11 Attack (7)
13 Fine linen (4)
15 Contradiction (6)
17 Not present (6)
20 Be gloomy (4)
22 Far station (7)
24 Fragment (5)
26 Animal (5)
27 Belly (7)
28 Predicament (7)
29 Ballads (5)

Down

1 Admonish (7)
2 Twelve (5)
3 Ape (7)
4 Bray (3-3)
5 Cables (5)
6 Butt in (7)
7 Core (5)
12 Come apart (4)
14 Donations (4)
16 Women's game (7)
18 Also (7)
19 News (7)
21 Capital of Canada (6)
22 Egg-shaped (5)
23 Narcotic (5)
25 Printing type (5)

Across

1 Interregnum administrators (7)
5 Free entertainment (5)
8 Ruched edging (5)
9 Venezuelan capital (7)
10 Cost (7)
11 Country house (5)
12 Afternoon nap (6)
14 Senselessness (6)
17 Of the city (5)
19 Horizontal beam (7)
22 Row of houses (7)
23 Crudely bright (5)
24 Estimated (5)
25 Bodily manipulator (7)

Down

1 Loot (5)
2 Brief sighting (7)
3 Artificial fibre (5)
4 Small packet (6)
5 Flourished (7)
6 Surpass (5)
7 Italian region (7)
12 Leisurely stroll (7)
13 Drinking vessel (7)
15 Abstruse (7)
16 Brook (6)
18 Brimless cap (5)
20 Old Scots county (5)
21 Municipal dignitary (5)

Across

1 Easy gallop (6)
4 Basque cap (5)
8 Deeply upset (3,2)
9 Kneecap (7)
10 Computer data (4-3)
11 Operatic solo (4)
12 Night before (3)
14 Gaiety (4)
15 Eastern language (4)
18 Flatfish (3)
21 Small island (4)
23 Sports person (7)
25 Lay claim (7)
26 Kingdom (5)
27 Late (5)
28 Brigand (6)

Down

1 Roman orator (6)
2 Game (7)
3 Given a job (8)
4 English spa (4)
5 Governor (5)
6 One for the pot (3-3)
7 Sudden flood (5)
13 Well-being (8)
16 Resistant to change (3-4)
17 Gasteropod (6)
19 Light wood (5)
20 Head protector (6)
22 Part of a church (5)
24 Tax (4)

Across

5 Grind one's teeth (5)
8 Contoured fields (8)
9 Great anger (5)
10 Paraphrased (8)
11 Far Eastern country (5)
14 Consumed (3)
16 Left unseeded (6)
17 Disorderly lout (6)
18 Fall behind (3)
20 Burglar's bar (5)
24 Supply with water (8)
25 Fine and plump (5)
26 Protect from cold (8)
27 Racecourse (5)

Down

1 Strict (5)
2 Doglike sound (5)
3 Bear (5)
4 Turn down (6)
6 Teller of tales (8)
7 Over satisfied (8)
12 Very hungry (8)
13 Long-legged bird (8)
14 Boring tool (3)
15 Unit of energy (3)
19 Notorious (6)
21 Resentment (5)
22 Non-Christian (5)
23 Postpone (5)

Across

1 Delirium tremens (7)
5 Spaciousness (5)
8 Refute (5)
9 Set free (7)
10 Nonconformist (9)
12 Acquire (3)
13 Thrashed (6)
14 Frightened (6)
17 Ensnare (3)
18 Sleepy (9)
20 Coming (7)
21 Bush (5)
23 Impetuous (5)
24 Keepsake (7)

Down

1 Women's quarters (5)
2 Bone (3)
3 Result (7)
4 Squalid (6)
5 Schism (5)
6 Fizzy drink (9)
7 Appointed (7)
11 Italian restaurant (9)
13 Below (7)
15 Floating wreckage (7)
16 Symbol (6)
18 Cabbage (5)
19 Forbidden (5)
22 Flow (3)

Across

1 Leads (5)
4 Necessitates (7)
8 Pensioned off (7)
9 Change (5)
10 Foremost (5)
11 Default (7)
13 Ship's company (4)
15 Detest (6)
17 Come out (6)
20 Land-measure (4)
22 Efficient (7)
24 Depart (5)
26 Coral island (5)
27 Strain (7)
28 Raise (7)
29 Artist's stand (5)

Down

1 Inimical (7)
2 Thespian (5)
3 Score (7)
4 Bear (6)
5 Educate (5)
6 Whole number (7)
7 Wait on (5)
12 Large jug (4)
14 Genuine (4)
16 Sanction (7)
18 Mixture (7)
19 Everlasting (7)
21 Middle (6)
22 Stop (5)
23 Light wood (5)
25 Zodiacal sign (5)

116

Across

1 Glossy (8)
7 Girl's name (5)
8 Drowsy (9)
9 Edible tuber (3)
10 Rancid (4)
11 Greek deity (6)
13 Jovial (6)
14 Tiresome (6)
17 Concealed, secret (6)
18 Organ of flight (4)
20 Regret (3)
22 Garrulous (9)
23 Egg-shaped (5)
24 Cases in point (8)

Down

1 Animal skins (5)
2 Salad vegetable (7)
3 Counterfeit (4)
4 Motor (6)
5 Eng. diarist (5)
6 Rodent (7)
7 Danger to shipping (7)
12 Common soldier (7)
13 Cigar (7)
15 Beginning (7)
16 Verbose (6)
17 Tree (5)
19 Conjecture (5)
21 Tranquil (4)

Across

7 Ball game (6)
8 Din (6)
10 Assuage (7)
11 Indian capital (5)
12 Final (4)
13 Simple song (5)
17 Courteous (5)
18 Heroic verse (4)
22 Dandy (5)
23 Greek 'u' (7)
24 Lay on (6)
25 Large wine bottle (6)

Down

1 Unfruitful (7)
2 Examine critically (7)
3 Nettle-rash (5)
4 Authoritative command (7)
5 Cranium (5)
6 Follower of Zeno (5)
9 Rabble-rousing (9)
14 Lacking purpose (7)
15 Affluent (7)
16 Frugality (7)
19 Savoury jelly (5)
20 Entice (5)
21 Academy Award (5)

Across

1 Substitute (5-2)
5 Mucous discharge (5)
8 Replanted (5)
9 Piece of mosaic (7)
10 Leopard (7)
11 Kingly (5)
12 Resolve (6)
14 Against (6)
17 Eyeshield (5)
19 Natural surroundings (7)
22 Vehicle (7)
23 Decreased (5)
24 Grasslike plant (5)
25 Effusive (7)

Down

1 Belt (5)
2 Poison (7)
3 Trench (5)
4 Essence (6)
5 Extra player (7)
6 Funeral-song (5)
7 Infectious disease (7)
12 Indirect (7)
13 Long-lasting (7)
15 Devilish (7)
16 Tool (6)
18 Church council (5)
20 Arbour (5)
21 —— wave (5)

Across

1 Wed (5)
4 Herb (5)
10 French painter (7)
11 Attach (5)
12 Wait on (5)
13 Impatient (7)
15 Cut (4)
17 Inscribe (5)
19 Cake-topping (5)
22 Sly (4)
25 Comfort (7)
27 Share out (5)
29 Corroborate (5)
30 Heir (7)
31 Edge (5)
32 Decorate (5)

Down

2 Thespian (5)
3 Esteem (7)
5 Piles (5)
6 Large house (7)
7 Entertain (5)
8 Paris underground (5)
9 Outshine (5)
14 Heroic (4)
16 Genuine (4)
18 Spite (7)
20 Altered (7)
21 Range (5)
23 Answer (5)
24 Precipitous (5)
26 Sea (5)
28 Afterwards (5)

120

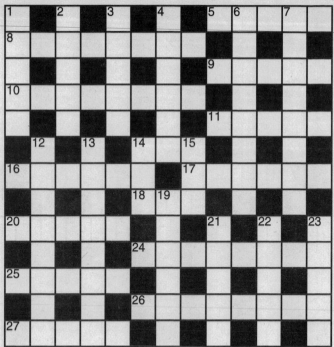

Across

5 Wooded ravine (5)
8 Bun-fight (3-5)
9 Quaintly amusing (5)
10 Insect (8)
11 Boundary (5)
14 Rainy (3)
16 Seafarer (6)
17 Public speaker (6)
18 Bark (3)
20 Cellar (5)
24 Game bird (8)
25 US state (5)
26 Form mental image of (8)
27 Commerce (5)

Down

1 Base of felled tree (5)
2 Lariat (5)
3 Worth (5)
4 Sculpture (6)
6 Scolding old woman (8)
7 Toffee on a stick (8)
12 Breed of dog (8)
13 Careless (8)
14 Askew (3)
15 Spinning toy (3)
19 Hasten (anag) (6)
21 Swift (5)
22 Waterway (5)
23 Guide vessel (5)

Across

1 Pillar (6)
4 Irish dramatist (5)
8 Licit (5)
9 Towed vehicle (7)
10 Dead skin (7)
11 Volcano (4)
12 Spider's trap (3)
14 Spoken (4)
15 Crime (4)
18 Work unit (3)
21 Aspiration (4)
23 Accept (7)
25 Sale (7)
26 Courageous (5)
27 Boundary (5)
28 Swift dish (6)

Down

1 Cotton cloth (6)
2 Boat (7)
3 Small particle (8)
4 Bill (4)
5 Slave (5)
6 Natural (6)
7 Scatter (5)
13 Critical remark (8)
16 Ape (7)
17 Flog (6)
19 Concede (5)
20 Ornament (6)
22 Walked (5)
24 Dance (4)

122

Across

1 Investigate (5)
4 Effervesce (6)
9 Naive (7)
10 Brute (5)
11 Cereal (4)
12 Feeling (7)
13 Pelt (3)
14 Threesome (4)
16 Rim (4)
18 Hostelry (3)
20 Oriental (7)
21 Brace (4)
24 Snow-house (5)
25 Nil (7)
26 Agreement (6)
27 Correct (5)

Down

1 Flatfish (6)
2 Aquatic animal (5)
3 Always (4)
5 Continuous (8)
6 Supporting (7)
7 Stretch (6)
8 Willow (5)
13 Leading (8)
15 Determine (7)
17 Withstand (6)
18 Silly (5)
19 Alarm (6)
22 Mimicking (5)
23 Agitate (4)

Across

1 In reserve (5)
4 Tyrannize (7)
8 Firing mechanism (7)
9 Tremble (5)
10 Peninsula of NE Egypt (5)
11 Heavy jersey (7)
13 Waist-band (4)
15 Zero (6)
17 Flowering shrub (6)
20 Avowal (4)
22 Wins over (7)
24 Kit out (5)
26 Cook in oven (5)
27 One more (7)
28 Fortress (7)
29 Austrian province (5)

Down

1 Skilled worker (7)
2 Mythical king bound to a wheel (5)
3 Language (7)
4 Female giant (6)
5 Resentment (5)
6 Stretchable (7)
7 Weapon (5)
12 Questioning word (4)
14 Small particle (4)
16 Parvenu (7)
18 Cigar (7)
19 Clothing (7)
21 Attack (6)
22 Style of architecture (5)
23 Assessed (5)
25 Court official (5)

Across

7 Farinaceous vegetable (6)
8 Bloom (6)
10 Censure (7)
11 Freight (5)
12 Declare false (4)
13 Preserving by salting (5)
17 Reluctance to work (5)
18 South Yemeni capital (4)
22 Confess (5)
23 Funeral mass (7)
24 Fleshy (6)
25 Black porcelain (6)

Down

1 Promote (7)
2 Clerical salary (7)
3 Bend over (5)
4 Make looser (7)
5 Blasphemed (5)
6 Conclusive evidence (5)
9 Unmethodical (9)
14 Floating wreckage (7)
15 Naval supremo (7)
16 Enliven (7)
19 Cheek (5)
20 Scornful smile (5)
21 Red Indian woman (5)

Across

7 Second-mentioned (6)
8 Masticated (6)
10 Odd (7)
11 Wash (5)
12 Unlock (4)
13 Tart fruit (5)
17 Tempest (5)
18 Tiny bird (4)
22 Grossly overweight (5)
23 Insignificant (7)
24 Whiten (6)
25 German composer (6)

Down

1 Flower (7)
2 Begun (7)
3 Casual wear (5)
4 Egyptian king (7)
5 Oscillate (5)
6 Viper (5)
9 Go through (9)
14 Elongate (7)
15 Cargo (7)
16 Eternal (7)
19 Uncertainty (5)
20 Gem (5)
21 Narrow inlet (5)

126

Across

1 Hair-dresser (6)
4 Line of people (5)
8 Money (5)
9 Disastrous (7)
10 Broke out (7)
11 Cow-shed (4)
12 Large deer (3)
14 Mock (4)
15 European mountain range (4)
18 Health resort (3)
21 Crazy (4)
23 Tail-ender (7)
25 Vine (7)
26 Wake up (5)
27 Tin-glazed earthenware (5)
28 Milk punch (6)

Down

1 Projectile (6)
2 Hermit (7)
3 Voters (8)
4 Leave (4)
5 Black timber (5)
6 Followed (6)
7 Family of lions (5)
13 Australian marsupial (8)
16 Epidemics (7)
17 Positioned (6)
19 Sudden fear (5)
20 Refer to (6)
22 Fish basket (5)
24 Roasting contrivance (4)

Across

1 Dandies (5)
4 Pretty girls (6)
9 Hotchpotch (7)
10 Poisonous (5)
11 Luxuriant (4)
12 Molasses (7)
13 Low (3)
14 Scheming (2,2)
16 Rabbit (4)
18 Tree (3)
20 Card game (7)
21 Diplomacy (4)
24 Ragout (5)
25 Annoying (7)
26 Oxfordshire town (6)
27 Stealing (5)

Down

1 Happen (6)
2 Tapestry (5)
3 Photograph (4)
5 Dig in (8)
6 Dictionary (7)
7 Nauseate (6)
8 Slogan (5)
13 Insect (8)
15 Bewildered (7)
17 Violated (6)
18 Protection (5)
19 Certify (6)
22 Sun-dried brick (5)
23 Comic sketch (4)

128

Across

1 Sylvan deity (5)
4 Illumination (5)
10 Under (7)
11 Rub out (5)
12 Senior member (5)
13 Unproven (7)
15 Lip (4)
17 Commerce (5)
19 Each one (5)
22 Lose colour (4)
25 Painters (7)
27 Rascal (5)
29 Immaculate (5)
30 Building (7)
31 Precipitous (5)
32 Coral island (5)

Down

2 Irritate (5)
3 Longed (7)
5 Lifeless (5)
6 Weightier (7)
7 Dwelling (5)
8 Gesture of indifference (5)
9 Prepared (5)
14 Require (4)
16 Adroit (4)
18 Fall back (7)
20 Decision (7)
21 Spear (5)
23 Very pale (5)
24 Cap (5)
26 Rationality (5)
28 Cook (5)

Across

1 Pursue (5)
4 Metric tons (6)
9 Small tool (7)
10 Trio (5)
11 Looked on (4)
12 Liken (7)
13 Enemy (3)
14 Monster (4)
16 Hurried (4)
18 Baby's bed (3)
20 Whip (7)
21 Alone (4)
24 Wash (5)
25 Learner (7)
26 Rest (6)
27 Singer (5)

Down

1 Type of nut (6)
2 Astound (5)
3 Sea-eagle (4)
5 Sanguine person (8)
6 Tell (7)
7 Nordic country (6)
8 Cost (5)
13 Courageous (8)
15 Mature (5-2)
17 Money-lender (6)
18 Discontinue (5)
19 Medico (6)
22 Sea (5)
23 Fair (4)

130

Across

1 South American country (5)
4 Meteorological conditions (7)
8 Flier (7)
9 Piece let in (5)
10 Royal house (5)
11 Dawdler (7)
13 Highest point (4)
15 Mob (6)
17 Obstruct (6)
20 In addition (4)
22 Very much (7)
24 Thicket (5)
26 Distressed (5)
27 State of rest (7)
28 Discourse (7)
29 Raising agent (5)

Down

1 Warrant (7)
2 Homeric poem (5)
3 Hold spellbound (7)
4 Trilled song (6)
5 Imitating (5)
6 Kidnap victim (7)
7 Estimated (5)
12 Alliance (4)
14 Series of changes (4)
16 Consecrated (7)
18 Derision (7)
19 Tastefully attired (7)
21 Words of a song (6)
22 Dutch cheese (5)
23 Formal designation (5)
25 Long-grained rice (5)

Across

1 Place of worship (6)
4 Ecuadoran capital (5)
8 Scottish landowner (5)
9 Dutch philosopher (7)
10 Strong grass (7)
11 Son of Isaac (4)
12 Unused (3)
14 Threesome (4)
15 Greek letter (4)
18 Antelope (3)
21 Effortless (4)
23 Down in price (7)
25 Scent (7)
26 Angry (5)
27 Laud (5)
28 Discussion (6)

Down

1 Fungus (6)
2 Soft shoe (7)
3 Grounded (anag.) (8)
4 Drop out (4)
5 Golf clubs (5)
6 Murky (6)
7 Midland university (5)
13 Trachea (8)
16 Keyboard composition (7)
17 Humans (6)
19 Encouraged (5)
20 Stick (6)
22 Small fish (5)
24 Sea-bird (4)

132

Across

1 Beauty contestant (5)
4 Climatic conditions (7)
8 Resolute and frugal (7)
9 Rescued (5)
10 Wood-turning tool (5)
11 Monarch (7)
13 Land area (4)
15 Shortage (6)
17 Arachnid (6)
20 East Anglian river (4)
22 Drafted anew (7)
24 Remain in readiness (5)
26 Big (5)
27 Fur trader (7)
28 Indicated (7)
29 Woollen fabric (5)

Down

1 Hurried (7)
2 Most insignificant (5)
3 Plead (7)
4 Victor (6)
5 Writer of fables (5)
6 Fluttered motionless (7)
7 Horseman (5)
12 Army dining room (4)
14 Chinese breed of dog (4)
16 Firedog (7)
18 Rural freeholder (7)
19 Gone to bed (7)
21 Joined together (6)
22 Governed (5)
23 Avoid (5)
25 Sufficient (5)

Across

1 Fine worsted yarn (6)
4 Flash of lightning (6)
7 Children's game (9)
9 Act (4)
10 Suspend (4)
11 Film of oil (5)
13 Unusual item (6)
14 Vigorous (6)
15 Brownish-red (6)
17 Lawsuit (6)
19 Bitter aromatic gum (5)
20 Animal skin (4)
22 Maple genus (4)
23 Come to light (9)
24 Opportune (6)
25 Grease (6)

Down

1 Vulture (6)
2 Timber (4)
3 Finally (6)
4 Singe (6)
5 Opulent (4)
6 Regal (6)
7 Sincere (9)
8 Wig (4-5)
11 Play guitar (5)
12 Two-masted vessel (5)
15 Rumour (6)
16 Australian city (6)
17 Hollow under the shoulder (6)
18 Slender (6)
21 Accurate (4)
22 Russian sea (4)

134

Across

7 Fails to catch (6)
8 Trounced (6)
10 Euphoria (7)
11 Name (5)
12 Observed (4)
13 Disquiet (5)
17 Additional (5)
18 Expensive (4)
22 Flower (5)
23 Pharmacist (7)
24 Serviceable (6)
25 Aquiescent (6)

Down

1 Enormous (7)
2 Got away (7)
3 Commence (5)
4 Occidental (7)
5 Country (5)
6 Below (5)
9 Wrong (9)
14 Instance (7)
15 Shortage (7)
16 Pig's foot (7)
19 Concerning (5)
20 Roamer (5)
21 Criminal (5)

Across

1 Eccentric type (5)
4 Composer of The Messiah (6)
9 Berkshire town (7)
10 Sound of metal (5)
11 Evict (4)
12 Meaning (7)
13 Digit (3)
14 Island (4)
16 Shade (4)
18 Professional charge (3)
20 Dotted shading (7)
21 Temporary settlement (4)
24 Keen (5)
25 Law (7)
26 Vehement speech (6)
27 Longest musical note (5)

Down

1 Case (6)
2 Gather together (5)
3 Fashion without needles (4)
5 Precise (8)
6 Cavalryman (7)
7 Papal representative (6)
8 With mouth wide open (5)
13 Modified (8)
15 Insolent laugh (7)
17 Viewpoint (6)
18 Banquet (5)
19 Globe (6)
22 Entertain (5)
23 Essayist (4)

136

Across

1 Perused (4)
3 Oily fish (8)
9 Flatulence (5)
10 Not touched (7)
11 Costa (3)
13 Solo speech (9)
14 Creature (6)
16 Without charge (6)
18 Insect repellent (9)
20 Sensational paper (3)
22 Pressing clothes (7)
23 Linguistic peculiarity (5)
25 Wobbled (8)
26 Epidermis (4)

Down

1 Be repeated (5)
2 Piercing tool (3)
4 Resembling a horse (6)
5 Country walker (7)
6 Helmsman (9)
7 Despondency (7)
8 Impure film (4)
12 Sulphur (9)
14 Designate (7)
15 Stupid (7)
17 Unmarried (6)
19 Heroic verse (4)
21 Street urchin (5)
24 Vex (3)

Across

7 Respiratory complaint (6)
8 Titillate (6)
10 Windfall (7)
11 Spring flower (5)
12 Smile broadly (4)
13 Contempt (5)
17 Poetry (5)
18 Present (4)
22 Bloodsucker (5)
23 Leave out (7)
24 Arm muscle (6)
25 Stays (6)

Down

1 Vegetable (7)
2 Understudy (5-2)
3 Correct (5)
4 Unsettle (7)
5 Dexterity (5)
6 Lure (5)
9 Ancestral (anag.) (9)
14 Maybe (7)
15 Ask for (7)
16 Keepsake (7)
19 Sphere (5)
20 Instruct (5)
21 Performer (5)

138

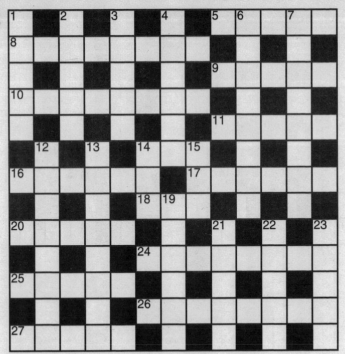

Across

5 Have the desire to (5)
8 Blue bell-shaped flower (8)
9 Jolly feast (5)
10 Rebound (8)
11 Injure with hot water (5)
14 Pig pen (3)
16 Wine flask (6)
17 Agreement (6)
18 Male cat (3)
20 Deadly (5)
24 Long dagger (8)
25 Sub-normal person (5)
26 Unique (8)
27 Perhaps (5)

Down

1 County (5)
2 Observe (5)
3 Minor difficulty (5)
4 Thoroughfare (6)
6 Looking gloomy (8)
7 Lambswool ointment (8)
12 Delusion of grandeur (8)
13 Underground cemetery (8)
14 Collection (3)
15 Tropical tuber (3)
19 Kit (6)
21 Poem (5)
22 Purloined (5)
23 Managing committee (5)

Across

1 Sandpiper (4)
3 Currents of air (8)
9 Welsh peninsula (5)
10 Robber (7)
11 Evergreen tree (3)
13 Highlander's cap (9)
14 Disconnect (6)
16 Glos town (6)
18 Pickled (9)
20 Stitch (3)
22 Small pill (7)
23 Shrink back (5)
25 Thick slice of bread (8)
26 Hit smartly (4)

Down

1 Ball-game (5)
2 Not many (3)
4 Hydrophobia (6)
5 Erect (7)
6 Extremely funny (9)
7 Wandered (7)
8 Fruit basket (4)
12 Aquatic ball-game (5-4)
14 Harmed (7)
15 Knock out (7)
17 Greek goddess (6)
19 Fine feathers (4)
21 Cereal plant (5)
24 Modern (3)

Across

1 Central-European (6)
4 Rowing crew (5)
8 Plenty (5)
9 Terse (7)
10 Imprecise (7)
11 Healthy (4)
12 Very warm (3)
14 Genuine (4)
15 Whirlpool (4)
18 consume (3)
21 Hasten (4)
23 Hospital social worker (7)
25 Old English author (7)
26 Din (5)
27 Gun (5)
28 Agree (6)

Down

1 Without charge (6)
2 Fully satisfied (7)
3 Compliant (8)
4 Every one (4)
5 Kind (5)
6 Amuse (6)
7 Fabric (5)
13 End of line (8)
16 Tooth-material (7)
17 Provision-merchant (6)
19 Linger (5)
20 Keen (6)
22 Office-workers (5)
24 Land-measure (4)

Across

1 Scottish firth (5)
4 Property (6)
9 Grant of rights (7)
10 Corporally punished (5)
11 Slightly wet (4)
12 Deep red (7)
13 Recline (3)
14 Pain (4)
16 Warty amphibian (4)
18 Purchase (3)
20 Sailing boat (7)
21 Work as a daily (4)
24 Tall building (5)
25 Protein forming horns etc (7)
26 Give employment to (6)
27 Heart beat (5)

Down

1 Architectural front (6)
2 Kingdom (5)
3 Intensely dislike (4)
5 Repository for vestments (8)
6 Loss of memory (7)
7 Conclusion (6)
8 Prayer before eating (5)
13 Vaulting game (8)
15 Idle conversation (7)
17 Mowing tool (6)
18 Wagonette (5)
19 Member of royal house (6)
22 Inn (5)
23 Support (4)

142

Across

1 Narrow channel (6)
4 Battles (6)
7 Example (9)
9 Influence (4)
10 Clutch (4)
11 Young eel (5)
13 Long for (6)
14 Lay waste (6)
15 Dementia (6)
17 Vacillate (6)
19 Lukewarm (5)
20 Barred enclosure (4)
22 Parched (4)
23 Sudden crisis (9)
24 Vigour (6)
25 Dozen (6)

Down

1 Pickled (6)
2 Breezy (4)
3 Lifting gear (6)
4 Animal feed (6)
5 Criminal mob (4)
6 Well-balanced (6)
7 Rectory (9)
8 Perfidy (9)
11 Upright (5)
12 Hydrophobic (5)
15 Site (6)
16 Annually (6)
17 Compendium (6)
18 Sieve (6)
21 Muslim governor (4)
22 Skin eruption (4)

Across

1 Quick look (4)
3 Region (8)
9 Uneven (5)
10 Small dressing (7)
11 Total (3)
13 Wrong (9)
14 Buccaneer (6)
16 Gathers (6)
18 Bedcover (9)
20 Look at (3)
22 Cover (7)
23 Midland town (5)
25 Amulet (8)
26 finest (4)

Down

1 Windproof jacked (5)
2 Flightless bird (3)
4 Bring from overseas (6)
5 Coach (7)
6 Reduction (anag.) (9)
7 Lunges (7)
8 Footwear (4)
12 Reckless person (9)
14 Monitor (7)
15 Chelonians (7)
17 Fair game (6)
19 Prison (sl.) (4)
21 Occasion (5)
24 Sheep (3)

144

Across

1 Lands (7)
5 Higher (5)
8 Church conference (5)
9 Disastrous (7)
10 Format (7)
11 Deduce (5)
12 Set down in detail (6)
14 Fine parchment (6)
17 Non-Christian (5)
19 Examiner of accounts (7)
22 Heavy labour (7)
23 Of same value (5)
24 Fine cotton thread (5)
25 Counters of money (7)

Down

1 Ancient Greek satirist (5)
2 Set fire to (7)
3 Shrubbery fence (5)
4 Twine (6)
5 Employ (7)
6 Trial print (5)
7 Speaking platform (7)
12 Main city (7)
13 Trumpeted welcome (7)
15 Salad vegetable (7)
16 Money purse (6)
18 Inform on colleagues (5)
20 Reside (5)
21 Small loaves (5)

Across

1 Chessman (6)
4 Characteristics (6)
7 Confectioners (5,4)
9 Pledge (4)
10 Maggot (4)
11 Buffoon (5)
13 Roof beam (6)
14 Surgical instrument (6)
15 Fan chaff from grain (6)
17 Outlaw (6)
19 More pleasant (5)
20 Fling up (4)
22 Front of a ship (4)
23 Remarkable sight (9)
24 Made proud (6)
25 Recently (6)

Down

1 Smoked herring (6)
2 Robe (4)
3 Shudder (6)
4 Tuft (6)
5 Eager (4)
6 Water-ice (6)
7 Speed (9)
8 Course of action (9)
11 Piece of stamped metal (5)
12 Method of detection (5)
15 Acacia (6)
16 Flinched (6)
17 Lament (6)
18 Gaudy (6)
21 Dot (4)
22 Conspiracy (4)

146

Across

1 Censure (7)
5 Waterside plant (5)
8 Sprite (5)
9 Wondrous (7)
10 Infinite (9)
12 Chart (3)
13 Underground room (6)
14 Far-off (6)
17 Evil (3)
18 Realise (9)
20 Cock (7)
21 Mistake (5)
23 Instructor (5)
24 Repletion (7)

Down

1 Urge on (5)
2 Annoy (3)
3 Lethargy (7)
4 Small village (6)
5 Wise men (5)
6 Rot (9)
7 Obscuration (7)
11 Clumsy (9)
13 Floor-show (7)
15 Highest mountain (7)
16 Games (6)
18 Change (5)
19 Filthy (5)
22 Regret (3)

Across

5 Appease (5)
8 Affrighted (8)
9 Trap (5)
10 Custom (8)
11 In reverse (5)
14 Expertise (3)
16 Great wave (6)
17 Alloy (6)
18 Weep (3)
20 Banish (5)
24 Atmosphere (8)
25 Town in Cornwall (5)
26 German motorway (8)
27 Vagrant (5)

Down

1 Proficient (5)
2 Composition (5)
3 Spiny plants (5)
4 Swordsman (6)
6 Deserted (8)
7 Breed of terrier (8)
12 Magician (8)
13 Plucking implement (8)
14 Curved line (3)
15 Plaything (3)
19 Canard (6)
21 Junior (5)
22 Skulk (5)
23 Coin (5)

148

Across

1 Father Christmas (5)
4 Talons (5)
10 Defame (7)
11 Perfect model (5)
12 Soothe (5)
13 Spotted (7)
15 Destitution (4)
17 Overgarments (5)
19 Time after time (5)
22 Proficient (4)
25 Non-professional (7)
27 Subsequently (5)
29 Porcelain (5)
30 Food colorant (7)
31 Register (5)
32 Computer language (5)

Down

2 Horrify (5)
3 Raging stream (7)
5 Telling untruths (5)
6 Come to grips (7)
7 Bring about (5)
8 Obtuse (5)
9 Forest clearing (5)
14 Carved image (4)
16 Isaac's son (4)
18 Prolonged applause (7)
20 Timorous (7)
21 Cheek (5)
23 Offensively self-assertive (5)
24 Mischievous trick (5)
26 Muse of love poetry (5)
28 Trunk (5)

Across

1 Profits (5)
4 Town division (7)
8 Parvenu (7)
9 Tenet (5)
10 Junior (5)
11 Sincere (7)
13 Kiln (4)
15 Hurled (6)
17 Public speaker (6)
20 Christen (4)
22 Heating (7)
24 Capital city (5)
26 Farewell (5)
27 Faint light (7)
28 Increase (7)
29 Panic (5)

Down

1 Epicure (7)
2 Norwegian dramatist (5)
3 Bird (7)
4 Takes a dip (6)
5 Codicil (5)
6 Ointment (7)
7 Core (5)
12 Minute particle (4)
14 Girl's name (4)
16 Staggering (7)
18 Facsimile (7)
19 Stage (7)
21 Descend (6)
22 Head-dress (5)
23 Colour (5)
25 Cuban dance (5)

150

Across

1 Period of polo play (7)
5 Utterly defeats (5)
8 Avoid (5)
9 Silent stage scene (7)
10 Unequalled (9)
12 Hastened (3)
13 Abrade (6)
14 Soap foam (6)
17 Beast of burden (3)
18 Swollen (9)
20 Supply with (7)
21 Dress cover (5)
23 Elevated line (5)
24 Shake (7)

Down

1 Demand as of right (5)
2 Feudal line in Orkney (3)
3 Sauce (7)
4 Preferably (6)
5 Name puzzle (5)
6 Dug up (9)
7 A good-looker (7)
11 Doorstep (9)
13 Run away (7)
15 Mean (7)
16 Declare (6)
18 Steer vehicle (5)
19 Poor student (5)
22 Steal (3)

Across

1 Public walk (4)
3 Do habitually (8)
9 Gem (5)
10 Seaport in NW Spain (7)
11 Groove (3)
13 Symbolise (9)
14 Manipulate (6)
16 Profoundly (6)
18 Purpose (9)
20 Tup (3)
22 Engraft (7)
23 Flimsy (5)
25 Collected (8)
26 Incentive (4)

Down

1 Greater (5)
2 Statute (3)
4 Cooking instructions (6)
5 Funeral procession (7)
6 Hotelier (9)
7 Just (7)
8 Aspersion (4)
12 Difficult situation (5,4)
14 Uniting (7)
15 Ancestry (7)
17 Goodness (6)
19 Tidings (4)
21 Chief officer (5)
24 Vital juice (3)

152

Across

1 Copper coins (5)
4 High ground (5)
10 Organise (7)
11 Depart (5)
12 Freight (5)
13 Adult (5-2)
15 Track (4)
17 Avid (5)
19 Decorate (5)
22 Monster (4)
25 Sea-god (7)
27 Assert (5)
29 Approximately (5)
30 Captain (7)
31 Fruit (5)
32 Stringed instrument (5)

Down

2 Mistake (5)
3 Comfort (7)
5 Snow-house (5)
6 Pupil (7)
7 Capture (5)
8 Rule (5)
9 Piles (5)
14 Back (4)
16 Press (4)
18 Sanction (7)
20 Delude (7)
21 Pummel (5)
23 Farmed birds (5)
24 Tingle (5)
26 Say (5)
28 Horrify (5)

Across

1 Rubbed to a shine (8)
7 Girl's name (5)
8 Sign of the zodiac (9)
9 Unwell (3)
10 Earth (4)
11 Consented (6)
13 Weapon (6)
14 Soul (6)
17 Glamour (6)
18 Speck of soot (4)
20 Total (3)
22 Slogan (9)
23 Opera by Puccini (5)
24 Donkey-work (8)

Down

1 Strides (5)
2 Plover (7)
3 Hide (4)
4 Sufficient (6)
5 Lukewarm (5)
6 Hermit (7)
7 Enrage greatly (7)
12 Carbon copy (7)
13 Thickness (7)
15 Pacify (7)
16 Author (6)
17 Entertain (5)
19 Drink (5)
21 Cast off (4)

154

Across

1 Battled (6)
4 Value (5)
8 MCC ground (5)
9 Utterly disorganised (7)
10 Distinguished (7)
11 Group of three (4)
12 Samuel's teacher (3)
14 Male admirer (4)
15 Taunt (4)
18 Despondent (3)
21 Pleasure-beach (4)
23 Wearing away (7)
25 Tenant farmer (7)
26 Pool (5)
27 Executing (5)
28 Code (6)

Down

1 Hesitate (6)
2 Soviet republic (7)
3 Evening star (8)
4 Debilitated (4)
5 Revolving arm (5)
6 Trojan commander (6)
7 Keen (5)
13 Disgrace (8)
16 Of the UK (7)
17 Calm (6)
19 Disparage (5)
20 Shackle (6)
22 Indian loincloth (5)
24 Market speculator (4)

Across

7 Breathing complaint (6)
8 Captivate (6)
10 Synthetic fibre (7)
11 Saturn satellite (5)
12 Row (4)
13 Skiff (5)
17 Sudden fright (5)
18 Support (4)
22 Transparent (5)
23 Commissioned rank (7)
24 Frolicsome (6)
25 Cut in two (6)

Down

1 Type of rummy (7)
2 First course (7)
3 Bouquet (5)
4 Made-up story (7)
5 Flatfish (5)
6 French river (5)
9 Metal for disposal (5-4)
14 Deep brown colour (7)
15 Carry on (7)
16 Conduct work (7)
19 Deceive (5)
20 Pungent (5)
21 Attach (5)

156

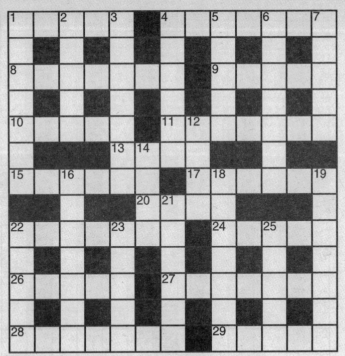

Across

1 Cut of beef (5)
4 Applaud (7)
8 Stately dance (7)
9 Utter (5)
10 Home planet (5)
11 Suffer from heat (7)
13 Large container (4)
15 County of N Ireland (6)
17 Stays (6)
20 Run with long strides (4)
22 Disease of malnutrition (7)
24 Body trunk (5)
26 Rapture (5)
27 Hiker (7)
28 Garden framework (7)
29 Town of NE France (5)

Down

1 Propose (7)
2 Baby eel (5)
3 Room for cooking (7)
4 Opposed (6)
5 Social class (5)
6 Criminally aided (7)
7 Manufacturer (5)
12 Bundle up (4)
14 Shoe seam (4)
16 Take delivery of (7)
18 Early (7)
19 Scottish pouch (7)
20 Egyptian god (6)
22 Automatic machine (5)
23 Painter's support (5)
25 Annoyed (5)

Across

1 Canopy (6)
4 Artifices (6)
7 Celestial being (9)
9 Floor covering (4)
10 Flesh used as food (4)
11 Vacillate (5)
13 Merchant (6)
14 Seldom (6)
15 Humorous (6)
17 Awkward (6)
19 Detested (5)
20 Conceited (4)
22 Love god (4)
23 Without doubt (9)
24 Footman (6)
25 Paradise (6)

Down

1 Memorial (6)
2 Novice (4)
3 Try again (6)
4 Ship (6)
5 Unit (4)
6 Slightly crazy (6)
7 S Polar region (9)
8 Fabulous (9)
11 Language (5)
12 Swift (5)
15 Joyous (6)
16 Coarse (6)
17 Fixation (6)
18 Sycophants (3-3)
21 Narrow part (4)
22 Charles Lamb (4)

158

Across

1 Line of people (5)
4 Heaviness (6)
9 Impressive (7)
10 Beneath (5)
11 Short letter (4)
12 Thai (7)
13 Mimic (3)
14 Very dry (4)
16 Gaelic (4)
18 Finish (3)
20 Thoughtful (7)
21 Behindhand (4)
24 On high (5)
25 Examine (7)
26 Pace (6)
27 Subsequently (5)

Down

1 Peculiar (6)
2 Upright (5)
3 Public school (4)
5 Trained (8)
6 Female deity (7)
7 Vegetable-dish (6)
8 Stop (5)
13 Confessed (8)
15 Malice (7)
17 Lances (6)
18 Weird (5)
19 Superior (6)
22 Representative (5)
23 Continent (4)

Across

1 Timpanist (7)
5 Milk-sop (5)
8 Yorkshire city (5)
9 Danger to shipping (7)
10 Arrest (9)
12 Bird (3)
13 Scoff (6)
14 Meal (6)
17 Note in tonic sol-fa scale (3)
18 Acerbic (9)
20 Yearly payment (7)
21 Girl's name (5)
23 Creed (5)
24 Nexus (7)

Down

1 Greek letter (5)
2 English river (3)
3 Transgression (7)
4 Marauder (6)
5 Great fear (5)
6 Awkward (9)
7 Milk-food (7)
11 Temple in Athens (9)
13 Far off (7)
15 Shoulder-ornament (7)
16 Chalk pencil (6)
18 Rapid (5)
19 Fissure (5)
22 Twosome (3)

160

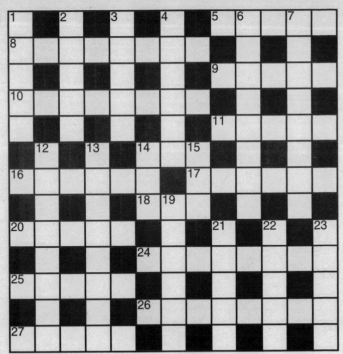

Across

5 Residence (5)
8 Thronging (8)
9 Legendary tale (5)
10 Oily (8)
11 Plunder (5)
14 Pigpen (3)
16 Term of office (6)
17 Bird enclosure (6)
18 Request (3)
20 Aquatic rodent (5)
24 Gambling attendant (8)
25 Spare-time interest (5)
26 Retarded (8)
27 Willow branch (5)

Down

1 Discharge (5)
2 Whim (5)
3 Love affair (5)
4 Inequitable (6)
6 Musical composition (8)
7 Beneficial (8)
12 Seemly (8)
13 Blameworthy (8)
14 Area of ocean (3)
15 Tibetan cattle (3)
19 Extend (6)
21 Fortunate (5)
22 Lombardic capital (5)
23 Vulgar (5)

Across

1 Strikes (6)
4 Moving parts (5)
8 Force out (5)
9 Betrothed (7)
10 Aromatic seed (7)
11 Even (4)
12 Cover (3)
14 Insect (4)
15 Egg-shaped (4)
18 Beverage (3)
21 Eastern language (4)
23 Allow (7)
25 Succeed (7)
26 Loved one (5)
27 Slacken (5)
28 Emphasise (6)

Down

1 Despicable person (6)
2 Painkiller (7)
3 Walk to it (anag.) (8)
4 Salary (4)
5 Bright star in Orion (5)
6 Calm (6)
7 Gem (5)
13 Crestfallen (8)
16 Flower (7)
17 Car protector (6)
19 Fruit of the oak (5)
20 Rubble (6)
22 Whimsical (5)
24 Highest point (4)

162

Across

7 Fast sailing boat (6)
8 Number (6)
10 Honest (7)
11 Middle Easterner (5)
12 Type of knot (4)
13 Indignation (5)
17 Extent (5)
18 Unconscious state (4)
22 Characteristic (5)
23 Follower of Christ (7)
24 Corroded (6)
25 Long flag (6)

Down

1 Come into possession of (7)
2 Hors d'oeuvre (7)
3 Wall of shrubs (5)
4 Least (7)
5 Wall painting (5)
6 Start (5)
9 Abyssinian (9)
14 Throw around (7)
15 Strive (7)
16 Wine (7)
19 Strict (5)
20 Middle part of body (5)
21 Wanderer (5)

Across

1 Thin fog (4)
3 In a gluey way (8)
9 Wild animal (5)
10 Able to be seen (7)
11 Scarlet (3)
13 Triple (9)
14 Football match (3-3)
16 Fished (6)
18 Force into service (5-4)
20 Tree (3)
22 Waterfall (7)
23 Cottage (5)
25 Walking with short steps (8)
26 Seethe (4)

Down

1 Gauge (5)
2 Droop (3)
4 Public house (6)
5 Water tank (7)
6 Confused mass (9)
7 Submitted (7)
8 Courage (4)
12 Sad (9)
14 Imitator (4-3)
15 Place in office (7)
17 Pothole (6)
19 Precious metal (4)
21 Mournful sound (5)
24 Couple (3)

164

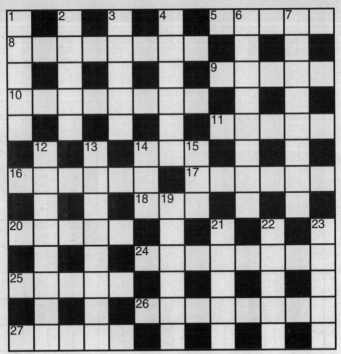

Across

5 Poison (5)
8 Ghosts (8)
9 Haggard (5)
10 Type of brandy (8)
11 Contact (5)
14 Allow (3)
16 Royal residence (6)
17 The East (6)
18 Man (3)
20 Read carefully (5)
24 Realm (8)
25 Investigate (5)
26 Nomad (8)
27 Subsequently (5)

Down

1 Attempt (5)
2 Appears (5)
3 Platform (5)
4 Ten years (6)
6 Musical composition (8)
7 Not guilty (8)
12 Germs (8)
13 Praiseworthy (8)
14 Support (3)
15 Plaything (3)
19 Commotion (6)
21 Dodge (5)
22 Irate (5)
23 Facial hair (5)

Across

1 Tie (6)
4 Detesting (6)
7 Boat with two hulls (9)
9 Metal (4)
10 Animal skin (4)
11 Aristocracy (5)
13 Antidote (6)
14 Wild (6)
15 Neglect (6)
17 Plant lacking in pigment (6)
19 Cavalry sword (5)
20 Noisy (4)
22 Wound (4)
23 Now and again (9)
24 Bashful (6)
25 Proficient (6)

Down

1 Digit (6)
2 Amphibian (4)
3 Almost (6)
4 Playing-card suit (6)
5 Snare (4)
6 Compassionate (6)
7 Insistent (9)
8 Villainous (9)
11 Borders (5)
12 Bird (5)
15 London district (6)
16 Aptitude (6)
17 Make good (6)
18 Costume (6)
21 Over (4)
22 Assist (4)

166

Across

1 Showering (7)
5 Sovereign (5)
8 Hymn of praise (5)
9 Equivocal (7)
10 Courteous regard (9)
12 Sick (3)
13 Avaricious (6)
14 Knight's jacket (6)
17 Hunter's haul (3)
18 Innocent (9)
20 Freedom from work (7)
21 Senseless (5)
23 Number below ten (5)
24 Curtly (7)

Down

1 Speedy (5)
2 Anger (3)
3 Disregarded (7)
4 Ecology party (6)
5 Tremble with fear (5)
6 Exterminate (9)
7 Irritated (7)
11 Young bird (9)
13 Gulped down (7)
15 Artist's studio (7)
16 Warning (6)
18 Unsharpened (5)
19 Run-down (5)
22 Reverence (3)

Across

1 Entire (5)
4 Mariners (7)
8 Border plant (7)
9 Ecological colour (5)
10 Change (5)
11 Completely (7)
13 Snatch (4)
15 American (6)
17 Pass, as time (6)
20 Type of bean (4)
22 Association (7)
24 Sweetener (5)
26 Correct (5)
27 Towing vessel (7)
28 After hostilities (4-3)
29 Room at the top (5)

Down

1 Small kangaroo (7)
2 Circuitous path (5)
3 Magnify (7)
4 Ancient Greek city (6)
5 Gold block (5)
6 A plover (anag.) (7)
7 Bright, cloudless (5)
12 Heed (4)
14 Be at ease (4)
16 Kernel (7)
18 Italian dish (7)
19 Spasmodic (7)
21 Bivalve (6)
22 Rascal (5)
23 Bequeath (5)
25 Phantom (5)

168

Across

1 Console (7)
5 Statistical chart (5)
8 Animal (5)
9 Let go (7)
10 Uprising (9)
12 Long period of time (3)
13 Season (6)
14 Light wind (6)
17 Thick-witted fellow (3)
18 Down-trodden (9)
20 Preserved (7)
21 Sub-continent (5)
23 Equestrian (5)
24 Diet (7)

Down

1 Tossing pole (5)
2 Extinct bird (3)
3 Small bird (7)
4 Sluggish (6)
5 Large claw (5)
6 Innocent (9)
7 Raise (7)
11 Unshaven (9)
13 Spy (7)
15 Drunk (7)
16 Arachnid (6)
18 Governor (5)
19 Pulled along (5)
22 Animal mother (3)

Across

1 Fragile (8)
7 German city (5)
8 Violent upheaval (9)
9 Regret (3)
10 Unusual (4)
11 Ensnare (6)
13 Yolk (6)
14 Painter's workshop (6)
17 Bird of prey (6)
18 Across (4)
20 Ben —— (3)
22 By degrees (9)
23 Liquid (5)
24 Disloyalty (8)

Down

1 Furnishings (5)
2 Sideways (7)
3 Male bird (4)
4 Irksome (6)
5 Seize forcibly (5)
6 Hell (7)
7 Chieftain's territory (7)
12 Study of animals (7)
13 Curdled dessert (7)
15 Witchcraft (7)
16 State of confidence (6)
17 Candid (5)
19 Regal (5)
21 Prickly seed-case (4)

170

Across

1 Short necklace (6)
4 Illumination (5)
8 Female relation (5)
9 Non-professional (7)
10 Obdurate (7)
11 Knock out (4)
12 Strike (3)
14 Depressed (4)
15 Confederate (4)
18 Noise (3)
21 Dutch cheese (4)
23 Letter (7)
25 Stuck (7)
26 Normal (5)
27 Strained (5)
28 Mean (6)

Down

1 Lively dance (6)
2 Protective wear (7)
3 Raised (8)
4 Burden (4)
5 Visitor (5)
6 Crowd (6)
7 Trust (5)
13 Uncommunicative (8)
16 Salad-stuff (7)
17 Leave (6)
19 Penurious (5)
20 Got better (6)
22 Very pale (5)
24 Gratis (4)

Across

1 Church official (6)
4 Scandinavian goblins (6)
7 Discomfit (9)
9 Sand-hill (4)
10 Flavour (4)
11 Morsel (5)
13 Fool (6)
14 Course through life (6)
15 Season (6)
17 Danish king of England (6)
19 Sacred book of Islam (5)
20 Glass (4)
22 Unfettered (4)
23 Doorsill (9)
24 Fur cape (6)
25 Hibernal (6)

Down

1 Benumb (6)
2 Arrive (4)
3 Shade of difference (6)
4 Road surfacing (6)
5 Hop-kiln (4)
6 Vocalist (6)
7 Delectation (9)
8 Precaution (9)
11 Glossy (5)
12 Heathen (5)
15 Hushed (6)
16 Eg squirrel (6)
17 Nut-tree (6)
18 Vigour (6)
21 Vessel (4)
22 Open tart (4)

172

Across

1 Making watertight (7)
5 Roof coverings (5)
8 Middle Easterner (5)
9 Accounts inspector (7)
10 Reckoning in tens (7)
11 Wading bird (5)
12 Hot spring (6)
14 Foul smell (6)
17 Modify (5)
19 Proselytizer (7)
22 Abstruse (7)
23 Animal life (5)
24 Large stove (5)
25 Agony (7)

Down

1 Discerned (5)
2 Political disorder (7)
3 Pelvic bone (5)
4 With pleasure (6)
5 Neatest (7)
6 Afterwards (5)
7 Withdraw from race (7)
12 Fascination (7)
13 Fire the interest (7)
15 Carved Japanese toggle (7)
16 Dormant (6)
18 Fire-raising (5)
20 Tender (5)
21 Precise (5)

Across

- **1** Male deer (4)
- **3** Waves (8)
- **9** Shelf (5)
- **10** Lauded (7)
- **11** Tree (3)
- **13** Lasting (9)
- **14** Fabric (6)
- **16** Be present (6)
- **18** Try (9)
- **20** Precious stone (3)
- **22** Spoke very slowly (7)
- **23** Cut off (5)
- **25** Bolster confidence (8)
- **26** Spa city (4)

Down

- **1** Divide in two (5)
- **2** Colour (3)
- **4** Give an account (6)
- **5** Unyielding (7)
- **6** Segregate (anag.) (6,3)
- **7** Tranquillised (7)
- **8** Cry (4)
- **12** Sensational play (9)
- **14** Cheese (7)
- **15** Dry Burgundy wine (7)
- **17** Consider (6)
- **19** Flower (4)
- **21** Jollity (5)
- **24** By way of (3)

174

Across

1 Agree (7)
5 Scolded (5)
8 Meeting-place (5)
9 Newness (7)
10 Shopkeeper (9)
12 Utter (3)
13 Rumpus (6)
14 Maintain (6)
17 Vapour (3)
18 Speed (9)
20 Tree-climbing animal (7)
21 Garden flower (5)
23 Rummage (5)
24 Attest (7)

Down

1 Group of witches (5)
2 Sister (3)
3 Precious stone (7)
4 Glitter (6)
5 Metal pin (5)
6 Optical instrument (9)
7 Tearless (3-4)
11 Capricious (9)
13 Sweetened (7)
15 Teacake (7)
16 Small fish (6)
18 Cite (5)
19 Cavity (5)
22 Pastry-lined dish (3)

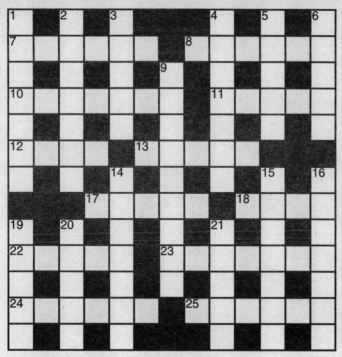

Across

7 Heaviness (6)
8 Former Tory Chairman (6)
10 Opposed to (7)
11 Fire-raising (5)
12 Peer (4)
13 Command (5)
17 Uncertainty (5)
18 Microbe (4)
22 Colour (5)
23 Wind instrument (7)
24 Stretch (6)
25 Acquiesce (6)

Down

1 Jumper (7)
2 Strange (7)
3 Gleam (5)
4 Retarded (7)
5 Grossly overweight (5)
6 Rock (5)
9 Trait (9)
14 Satisfied (7)
15 Non-plus (7)
16 Copy (7)
19 Rapidity (5)
20 Same (5)
21 Money-bag (5)

176

Across

1 Macabre (8)
7 Gives way (5)
8 Cliff face (9)
9 Antelope (3)
10 Osculate (4)
11 Fish (6)
13 Counterpart (6)
14 Overcoat (6)
17 Matelot (6)
18 Capital of South Yemen (4)
20 Spirit (3)
22 Plant (9)
23 Undersized (5)
24 Sovereign's daughter (8)

Down

1 Russian dance (5)
2 Tool (7)
3 Earth (4)
4 For the most part (6)
5 Proverb (5)
6 Life underwriter (7)
7 Character placed under a C (7)
12 Reasonable (7)
13 Flower-seller (7)
15 Larva of frog (7)
16 Nobody, the diarist (6)
17 Smudge (5)
19 Necessities (5)
21 Glance over (4)

Across

7 Engaged in battle (6)
8 Raps (6)
10 Trade restriction (7)
11 On a par (5)
12 Stole (4)
13 Trepidation (5)
17 Suspicious (5)
18 Nil (4)
22 Go into (5)
23 Retribution (7)
24 Light red (6)
25 Boarding-house warden (6)

Down

1 Personal belongings (7)
2 Wellington (7)
3 Entrance (5)
4 Vehement (7)
5 College servant (5)
6 Sacred song (5)
9 Smuggled liquor (9)
14 Wander off the point (7)
15 Harsh criticism (7)
16 Unexpected boon (7)
19 Two-masted boat (5)
20 Desolate (5)
21 Bedaub (5)

178

Across

1 Attractive sight (6)
4 Rise above (5)
8 Ensnare (5)
9 Arcadian (7)
10 Make ready (7)
11 Imperial title (4)
12 Label (3)
14 Greek letter (4)
15 Irritation (4)
18 Zodiac sign (3)
21 Stop (4)
23 Means of access (7)
25 Endurance (7)
26 Subject (5)
27 Produce (5)
28 Wild feline (6)

Down

1 Get away (6)
2 Ultimate limit (7)
3 Violent disturbance (8)
4 Playthings (4)
5 Dance (5)
6 Disc (6)
7 Asian land (5)
13 Enormous (8)
16 Hide (7)
17 Spirit (6)
19 High seas (5)
20 Most senior (6)
22 Depart (5)
24 Untamed (4)

Across

1 Ancient war vehicle (7)
5 Rips (5)
8 Group of eight (5)
9 Cartilage (7)
10 Prepared to resist attack (9)
12 Irritate (3)
13 Levelling board (6)
14 Debated (6)
17 Primate (3)
18 Wholly innocent (9)
20 Excuse (7)
21 Lazy fellow (5)
23 Estimated (5)
24 Boating event (7)

Down

1 Mob (5)
2 Piece of legislation (3)
3 Concentrated (7)
4 Mesopotamian river (6)
5 Tough string (5)
6 Characteristic (9)
7 Crept silently (7)
11 Stuffing (9)
13 Run away quickly (7)
15 Stinking (7)
16 Cold season (6)
18 Avarice (5)
19 Middle Eastern state (5)
22 One's fortune (3)

180

Across

1 Pepper (5)
4 If (7)
8 Surgical knife (7)
9 Threescore (5)
10 Conceptual (5)
11 Pointed tower (7)
13 Rock (4)
15 Steering device (6)
17 Set on fire (6)
20 Level (4)
22 Forgive (7)
24 Flag (5)
26 Seize forcibly (5)
27 Subject to duty (7)
28 Fugitive (7)
29 Clothes (5)

Down

1 Dismiss (7)
2 Furious (5)
3 Impetus (7)
4 Solidarity leader (6)
5 Happen later (5)
6 Animal with six feet (7)
7 Verse (5)
12 Yorkshireman (4)
14 Small bird (4)
16 Prison cell (7)
18 Linked (7)
19 Declare (7)
21 Church room (6)
22 Cringe (5)
23 Being pulled (2,3)
25 Card game (5)

Across

1 Letting fall (8)
7 Even up (5)
8 Sprightly (9)
9 Solemn promise (3)
10 Mountain lake (4)
11 Recess (6)
13 Austrian capital (6)
14 Haphazardly (6)
17 Resuscitate (6)
18 Discount (4)
20 Pair (3)
22 Donee (9)
23 Twisted (5)
24 Large fish (8)

Down

1 Piece of turf (5)
2 Head of a coin (7)
3 Bundle (4)
4 Simpleton (6)
5 Riddle (5)
6 Specialised skill (4-3)
7 Bewilder (7)
12 Dishonesty (7)
13 Flemish painter (7)
15 Sanitation (7)
16 Wading bird (6)
17 Spherical (5)
19 Many times (5)
21 Stout pole (4)

182

Across

7 Loftier (6)
8 Loftier (6)
10 Stir (7)
11 Vacant (5)
12 Row (4)
13 Artfulness (5)
17 Soup (5)
18 Ceremonial dress (4)
22 Cereal (5)
23 Nil (7)
24 Less difficult (6)
25 Rue (6)

Down

1 Italian wine (7)
2 Lit (7)
3 Rot (5)
4 Kneecap (7)
5 Slant (5)
6 Makes asinine sound (5)
9 Disinclined (9)
14 Spanish aristocrat (7)
15 Tree-shaping (7)
16 Heavy (7)
19 Concur (5)
20 Hesitate (5)
21 Precipitous (5)

183

Across

1 Hue (6)
4 Loosen (5)
8 Aroma (5)
9 Squeeze (7)
10 Masterly (7)
11 Woe is me! (4)
12 Family (3)
14 Norse god (4)
15 Relaxed (4)
18 Joke (3)
21 Dwelling (4)
23 Custom, procedure (7)
25 Departure (7)
26 Rumour (2,2)
27 Eng. city (5)
28 Belgian port (6)

Down

1 Alternative (6)
2 Big cat (7)
3 Rebellion (8)
4 Egg on (4)
5 Aggregate (5)
6 Man's name (6)
7 Merchandise (5)
13 Cloudy (8)
16 Bilk (7)
17 Hand-tool (6)
19 Transplant (5)
20 Group of five (6)
22 Church house (5)
24 Superintendent (4)

184

Across

1 Brunette (5)
4 Clerical incumbent (6)
9 Thai (7)
10 Accumulate (5)
11 Fail to include (4)
12 Heighten (7)
13 Mongrel (3)
14 Goddess of marriage (4)
16 Wild goat (4)
18 Assistance (3)
20 Poster (7)
21 Holdall (4)
24 Antelope (5)
25 Kneecap (7)
26 Dismal (6)
27 Blended (5)

Down

1 Massachusetts capital (6)
2 African ruminant (5)
3 Require (4)
5 Spider (8)
6 Apprentice (7)
7 Slice of bacon (6)
8 Cut off (5)
13 Strainer (8)
15 Ignorant (7)
17 Supported (6)
18 Expert (5)
19 High ground (6)
22 Take it easy (5)
23 Staunch (4)

Across

5 Correspond (5)
8 Clergyman (8)
9 Stink (5)
10 Clamber (8)
11 Trap (5)
14 Weep (3)
16 Desk (6)
17 Range (6)
18 Encountered (3)
20 French city (5)
24 Ovation (8)
25 Fabricate (5)
26 Fearless (8)
27 Hotel (5)

Down

1 Grip (5)
2 Public (5)
3 Muscle pain (5)
4 Fisherman (6)
6 Chew the cud (8)
7 Broad-minded (8)
12 Meddler (8)
13 Youth (8)
14 Combined with (3)
15 Again (3)
19 Dilate (6)
21 Look fiercely (5)
22 Infectious disease (5)
23 Italian composer (5)

186

Across

1 Water source (6)
4 Wearied by repetition (5)
8 Large stream (5)
9 Cleft (7)
10 Wealth (7)
11 Average (4)
12 Sharp tap (3)
14 Lake (4)
15 English flower (4)
18 Immerse (3)
21 Curved gateway (4)
23 French holiday area (7)
25 Catholic school (7)
26 Part of target (5)
27 Cattle farm (5)
28 Climb (6)

Down

1 Conflict (6)
2 Day dream (7)
3 Fed and brought up (8)
4 Fish (4)
5 Itinerary (5)
6 Governess (6)
7 Subsequently (5)
13 Earlier (8)
16 Ghost (7)
17 Native seaman (6)
19 Boast (5)
20 Prohibited (6)
22 Cathedral dignitary (5)
24 Network (4)

Across

1 Requests (5)
4 Place of study (7)
8 Power (7)
9 Of the eye (5)
10 Great (5)
11 Tumbler (7)
13 N Wales resort (4)
15 Boy's name (6)
17 Stress (6)
20 Lady (4)
22 Very dear (7)
24 S American animal (5)
26 Make merry (5)
27 Mythical animal (7)
28 Autumn festival (7)
29 Characteristic manner (5)

Down

1 Well-liked (7)
2 Consumer (5)
3 Genuine (7)
4 Nevertheless (6)
5 Love-affair (5)
6 Edible (7)
7 Sailing boat (5)
12 Shellfish (4)
14 London park (4)
16 Set free (7)
18 Temperature scale (7)
19 Learner (7)
21 Regulate (6)
22 Origin (5)
23 Regulating device (5)
25 Great pain (5)

188

Across

1 Set (5)
4 Ancient twisted neckband (6)
9 Hopelessness (7)
10 Sentry (5)
11 Melody (4)
12 Cathedral (7)
13 Bashful (3)
14 Gravel (4)
16 Certain (4)
18 Anthropoid (3)
20 Bill (7)
21 Festival (4)
24 Fetch (5)
25 Examine (7)
26 Football team (6)
27 Change (5)

Down

1 Self-possessed (6)
2 Norwegian dramatist (5)
3 Dutch cheese (4)
5 Put in order (8)
6 Fourth (7)
7 Tolerate (6)
8 Dirty (5)
13 Contend (8)
15 Lie back (7)
17 White stone (6)
18 Upper room (5)
19 Court clown (6)
22 Upright (5)
23 Continent (4)

Across

1 Ice over (6)
4 Fruit (5)
8 Flower (5)
9 Gallantry (7)
10 Wise (7)
11 Slight advantage (4)
12 Deer (3)
14 "The Abominable Snowman" (4)
15 Whirlpool (4)
18 Short sleep (3)
21 Wander (4)
23 Blow up (7)
25 Brimstone (7)
26 Wideawake (5)
27 Wild West show (5)
28 Antidote (6)

Down

1 Fixation (6)
2 Blot out (7)
3 Airship (8)
4 Recreation (4)
5 In the lead (5)
6 Tomboy (6)
7 Diminish (5)
13 Souvenir (8)
16 Bishop's district (7)
17 India-rubber (6)
19 Gem (5)
20 Guard (6)
22 Authentic, in force (5)
24 US state (4)

190

Across

- **1** Habitation (5)
- **4** Conjectured (7)
- **8** Shrink (7)
- **9** Thespian (5)
- **10** Stratum (5)
- **11** Separate from others (7)
- **13** Religious denomination (4)
- **15** Place of exit (6)
- **17** Emphasise (6)
- **20** Debauched revel (4)
- **22** Toilet-water (7)
- **24** Approximately (5)
- **26** Inflexible (5)
- **27** Minoan capital (7)
- **28** Perceive (7)
- **29** Derby venue (5)

Down

- **1** Minor Spanish noble (7)
- **2** Become one (5)
- **3** Sanction (7)
- **4** Erse (6)
- **5** Muse of love poetry (5)
- **6** Locate (7)
- **7** Funereal lamentation (5)
- **12** Market speculator (4)
- **14** Famous school (4)
- **16** Corresponds (7)
- **18** Violent hurricane (7)
- **19** Horizontal beam (7)
- **21** Calculate (6)
- **22** Boxed (5)
- **23** Faux pas (5)
- **25** Hazards (5)

Across

1 More fleshy (7)
5 Religious observances (5)
8 Circumference (5)
9 Seaman (7)
10 Restraint (7)
11 Urge forward (5)
12 Avaricious (6)
14 Aircraft shed (6)
17 Lively (5)
19 Violent storm (7)
22 Raffle (7)
23 Strange (5)
24 Distinctive character (5)
25 Pity (7)

Down

1 Conjuring (5)
2 Organise (7)
3 Watery humour (5)
4 Low, rolling noise (6)
5 Greek wine (7)
6 Spring flower (5)
7 Colonist (7)
12 Antelope (7)
13 Aridity (7)
15 River of ice (7)
16 Supporter (6)
18 Plot of ground (5)
20 Empire (5)
21 Snow-leopard (5)

192

Across

7 Cream product (6)
8 Instant (6)
10 Fail to care for (7)
11 Hangman's loop (5)
12 Possesses (4)
13 Lorry (5)
17 Young mare (5)
18 Lebanese port (4)
22 Forthright (5)
23 Tinned fish (7)
24 Limb brace (6)
25 Bog (6)

Down

1 Leave (7)
2 Planks for platform (7)
3 Dissuade (5)
4 Unite (7)
5 Criminal (5)
6 Riding horse (5)
9 Cleanse of germs (9)
14 Session (7)
15 Inclined to disbelieve (7)
16 Death (7)
19 Misuse (5)
20 Pugnacious type (5)
21 Ponder mournfully (5)

Across

1 Went on horseback (4)
3 Brushing (8)
9 Poison (5)
10 Dumplings (7)
11 Lick up (3)
13 Town in Kent (9)
14 Rich (6)
16 Greek goddess (6)
18 Workplace (9)
20 Ram (3)
22 Alerted (anag.) (7)
23 New (5)
25 Men of letters (8)
26 Underworld river (4)

Down

1 Competitor (5)
2 Lair (3)
4 Tepee (6)
5 Wearing away (7)
6 Increase (9)
7 Hot plate (7)
8 Complacent (4)
12 Widespread (9)
14 Principal city (7)
15 Bullfighter (7)
17 Take willingly (6)
19 Wild-cat (4)
21 Garden flower (5)
24 Examine (3)

194

Across

1 Fortification ditch (5)
4 High ground (5)
10 Get better (7)
11 Dire (5)
12 Mistake (5)
13 Great Lakes port (7)
15 Old (4)
17 Pleasant expression (5)
19 Faux pas (5)
22 Waterside plant (4)
25 Predicament (7)
27 Debate (5)
29 Bury (5)
30 Scrutinise (7)
31 Harbour (5)
32 Aquatic animal (5)

Down

2 Happen (5)
3 Few (7)
5 Unsuitable (5)
6 Successful launch (4-3)
7 Short (5)
8 Self-satisfaction (5)
9 Wind instrument (5)
14 Rim (4)
16 Bacillus (4)
18 Non-professional soldiers (7)
20 Inflexible (7)
21 Allow in (5)
23 Avid (5)
24 Cut (5)
26 Amalgamate (5)
28 Lead (5)

Across

1 Girl's name (5)
4 Uttered cry of a horse (7)
8 Passive ill-treated person (7)
9 Hector (5)
10 Italian explorer (5)
11 Unduly high offer (7)
13 Sea eagle (4)
15 Go to bed (6)
17 Northern ocean (6)
20 Unaccompanied (4)
22 Frivolous (7)
24 Brown pigment (5)
26 Fleshy flap at back of throat (5)
27 Anguish (7)
28 Voter (7)
29 Junior (5)

Down

1 Cocktail (7)
2 Lozenge-shaped object (5)
3 Rodent (7)
4 Idea (6)
5 Instil, permeate (5)
6 Fish (7)
7 Wood-nymph (5)
12 Flesh of calf (4)
14 Relax (4)
16 Accolade (7)
18 Conductor's platform (7)
19 Prattle (7)
21 Shellfish (6)
22 Stroke of luck (5)
23 core (5)
25 Prettify (5)

196

Across

1 Stove (6)
4 Main meal (6)
7 Vain (9)
9 Cooking fat (4)
10 Impress deeply (4)
11 Yugoslavian currency (5)
13 Distinction (6)
14 Sitting (6)
15 University examinations (6)
17 Japanese hostess (6)
19 Sum (5)
20 Ultimate (4)
22 Den (4)
23 Withdrawal (9)
24 Heated (6)
25 Compendium (6)

Down

1 Underground store (6)
2 Nomadic Turk (4)
3 Dried grape (6)
4 Texan city (6)
5 Olefactory organ (4)
6 Moved swiftly (6)
7 Candour (9)
8 Prominent politician (9)
11 Resided (5)
12 Insurgent (5)
15 Uncultivated (6)
16 Stained (6)
17 Asphyxiated (6)
18 Curt (6)
21 Limited period (4)
22 Yearn (4)

Across

1 Precious stone (5)
4 Manipulate (7)
8 Free (7)
9 Sea-birds (5)
10 Moulds (5)
11 This sum (anag.) (7)
13 Vow (4)
15 Rectangle (6)
17 Work produced (6)
20 Flat (4)
22 Meet head-on (7)
24 Fantasy (5)
26 Florida resort (5)
27 Particular (7)
28 Cut glass (7)
29 Goatlike deity (5)

Down

1 Jordanian town (7)
2 Cathedral city (5)
3 Relationship (7)
4 Attribute (6)
5 Hours of darkness (5)
6 Type of herring fillet (7)
7 Endures (5)
12 Footwear (4)
14 Very old (4)
16 Cradle song (7)
18 Disrobe (7)
19 Acrobat (7)
21 Container (6)
22 Humorous (5)
23 Foolish person (5)
25 Decree (5)

198

Across

1 Retail businesses (5)
4 Lubricated (5)
10 Imply (7)
11 Royal family (5)
12 Temporary peace (5)
13 Made of earthenware (7)
15 Concept (4)
17 Make up for (5)
19 Fishing vessel (5)
22 Brief letter (4)
25 Card game (7)
27 Uncertainty (5)
29 Great danger (5)
30 Slope (7)
31 Impolite grin (5)
32 Fast of foot (5)

Down

2 Native of India (5)
3 Food component (7)
5 Bury (5)
6 Locally prevalent (7)
7 Antarctic explorer (5)
8 Tranquillity (5)
9 Split open (5)
14 Orient (4)
16 Surface depression (4)
18 Fit of petulance (7)
20 Health examination (7)
21 Extent (5)
23 Desert haven (5)
24 Soak (5)
26 Relating to the sun (5)
28 Combine (5)

Across

1 Narrow at sea (6)
4 Raised anchor (6)
7 Furious (9)
9 Pit (4)
10 Poetic name for Ireland (4)
11 Unsheltered (5)
13 Wig (6)
14 Fluid (6)
15 Statue base (6)
17 Run aground (6)
19 Evergreen shrub (5)
20 Smudge (4)
22 Prejudice (4)
23 Inducing sleep (9)
24 Reddish element (6)
25 Concealed (6)

Down

1 Give in (6)
2 Skin disease (4)
3 Small amount (6)
4 Yearly (6)
5 Sea-eagle (4)
6 With antlers (6)
7 Harmful (9)
8 Emotionally shocking (9)
11 Bed on board (5)
12 Pool (5)
15 Generally known (6)
16 Glory (6)
17 Toboggan (6)
18 Plan (6)
21 Gambol (4)
22 Attach (4)

200

Across

1 More remote (7)
5 Herb (5)
8 Maturer (5)
9 Calculate (7)
10 Everlasting (7)
11 Yellow colouring (5)
12 Afternoon rest (6)
14 Wooden hammer (6)
17 Repeatedly (5)
19 Freedom (7)
22 Outdo (7)
23 Much overweight (5)
24 Modify (5)
25 Breed of dog (7)

Down

1 Compel (5)
2 Fully satisfied (7)
3 River bird (5)
4 Remember (6)
5 Lottery (7)
6 Lad (5)
7 Highest mountain (7)
12 Welsh port (7)
13 Beer-glass (7)
15 Theft (7)
16 Shuts (6)
18 Concur (5)
20 Flower (5)
21 Cede (5)

Across

7 3 miles (6)
8 Confederates (6)
10 Bulletin (7)
11 Of birth (5)
12 Old work for 'enough' (4)
13 Harbour (5)
17 Mad (5)
18 Complacent (4)
22 Flower (5)
23 Dig up (7)
24 Abandon (6)
25 Russian port (6)

Down

1 Mountaineer (7)
2 Large house (7)
3 Of the moon (5)
4 Menial servant (7)
5 Piebald horse (5)
6 Sacred song (5)
9 Unshakable (9)
14 Whaling weapon (7)
15 Print (7)
16 Intellectual (7)
19 Baffle (5)
20 Distress signal (5)
21 Prepared (5)

202

Across

1 Tomboy (6)
4 Indian monotheists (5)
8 Correspond (5)
9 Scholarly (7)
10 Rustled (7)
11 Fervour (4)
12 Weird (3)
14 Knock senseless (4)
15 Muslim leader (4)
18 Gratuity (3)
21 Dull pain (4)
23 Hansen's disease (7)
25 Agony (7)
26 Pledge of faith (5)
27 True-hearted (5)
28 Engraver (6)

Down

1 Funeral car (6)
2 White rose supporter (7)
3 Tusked mammal (8)
4 Complacent (4)
5 Cutting utensil (5)
6 Fitting (6)
7 Japanese fencing (5)
13 Journalistic report (8)
16 Concupiscent (7)
17 Artist's crayon (6)
19 Underworld god (5)
20 Code (6)
22 Grasping creature (5)
24 Cut down (4)

Across

1 Protection (7)
5 Riddle (5)
8 Corrupt (5)
9 Go to press (7)
10 Paint solvent (7)
11 Another time (5)
12 Tough (6)
14 Opportunity (6)
17 Heavenly body (5)
19 Pantomime character (7)
22 Italian wine (7)
23 Snarl (5)
24 Choose (5)
25 Small cucumber (7)

Down

1 Quilt (5)
2 Evasiveness (7)
3 Man-made fibre (5)
4 Skilled (6)
5 Rest day (7)
6 Heather (5)
7 Embellish (7)
12 Process for further use (7)
13 Defunct (7)
15 English county (7)
16 Season (6)
18 Cereal (5)
20 Bird of prey (5)
21 Claw (5)

Across

5 English county (5)
8 Informed (8)
9 Speed (5)
10 Part of a number (8)
11 Wild fruit (5)
14 House animal (3)
16 Suave (6)
17 Belgian port (6)
18 God of the woods (3)
20 Once more (5)
24 Invent idea of (8)
25 Face guard (5)
26 Topmost point (8)
27 Room for writing (5)

Down

1 Grampian town (5)
2 Small fish (5)
3 Scottish inlet (5)
4 Distant (6)
6 Egg dish (8)
7 Becoming narrower (8)
12 Pharmacist (8)
13 Many (8)
14 Tax-free investment (3)
15 Weight (3)
19 Handsome man (6)
21 In short supply (5)
22 Level of note (5)
23 Intoxicating nut (5)

Across

1 Disciple (5)
4 Uncertainty (5)
10 Compensate (7)
11 Shaver (5)
12 Dog (5)
13 Decamp (7)
15 Skilfully (4)
17 Pair (5)
19 Moroccan capital (5)
22 Oblique (4)
25 Dressmaker (7)
27 Meat cooked on a skewer (5)
29 Fortunate (5)
30 Hard rock (7)
31 Fool (5)
32 Counted up (5)

Down

2 Senior (5)
3 Mournful (7)
5 Gold lace (5)
6 Rocket launcher (7)
7 Neck injury (5)
8 Normal (5)
9 Vanity (5)
14 Cowshed (4)
16 Most excellent (4)
18 Diminished (7)
20 Ungainly (7)
21 Leisurely walk (5)
23 Small anchor (5)
24 Priory (5)
26 Authority (3-2)
28 Newly-wed (5)

206

Across

1 More tranquil (6)
4 Illumination (5)
8 Rub out (5)
9 Non-professional (7)
10 Cowboy (7)
11 Inactive (4)
12 Yelp (3)
14 Paradise (4)
15 Stone (4)
18 Gratuity (3)
21 Requests (4)
23 Elucidate (7)
25 Gift (7)
26 Wear away (5)
27 Horseman (5)
28 Mediterranean island (6)

Down

1 Stoned fruit (6)
2 Erudite (7)
3 Pachyderm (8)
4 Burden (4)
5 Avarice (5)
6 Vegetable dish (6)
7 Bear (5)
13 Foretell (8)
16 Uproar (7)
17 Meddle (6)
19 Unimportant (5)
20 Goes in (6)
22 Pummel (5)
24 Back (4)

Across

1 Give satisfaction (6)
4 Silver (6)
7 Yielding (9)
9 Mend (4)
10 Fight for breath (4)
11 Fish (5)
13 Explosion (6)
14 Fatuous smile (6)
15 Lustre (6)
17 Very small (6)
19 Lukewarm (5)
20 Incline (4)
22 Sleazy bar (4)
23 Dramatic actor (9)
24 Climax (6)
25 Over there (6)

Down

1 Mull over (6)
2 Soon (4)
3 Masterly (6)
4 Hostility (6)
5 Percussion instrument (4)
6 Meddle (6)
7 Intemperate (9)
8 Waterproofed canvas sheet (9)
11 Reliance (5)
12 Faint-hearted (5)
15 Hoi polloi (6)
16 Rows of shrubs (6)
17 Noon (6)
18 Admin. centre of Devon (6)
21 Malayan knife (4)
22 Daybreak (4)

208

Across

1 Set of links (5)
4 Skin eruptions (5)
10 Fir hunter (7)
11 Wild feline (5)
12 Theatre attendant (5)
13 Victorian novelist (7)
15 Religious picture (4)
17 Pastoral poem (5)
19 Tea container (5)
22 Seaweed jelly (4)
25 Tooth tissue (7)
27 Political clique (5)
29 Ottoman governor (5)
30 American lawman (7)
31 Sarcastic pessimist (5)
32 Mendacious (5)

Down

2 Common (5)
3 Endanger (7)
5 Spirit dispenser (5)
6 Intellectual (7)
7 Swagger (5)
8 Statement of belief (5)
9 Extremely stupid (5)
14 Peruvian Indian (4)
16 Familial tribe (4)
18 Ruling family (7)
20 Toxophily (7)
21 Skilful (5)
23 Plaster of Paris (5)
24 Simulate confidence (5)
26 Middle Easterner (5)
28 Scottish child (5)

Across

7 Fear (6)
8 Arm joints (6)
10 Gigantic (7)
11 Encourage (5)
12 Recess (4)
13 Transient (5)
17 Rodent (5)
18 Healthy (4)
22 Walker (5)
23 Disclose (7)
24 Tune (6)
25 Ball game (6)

Down

1 Endurance (7)
2 Deep red (7)
3 Punctuation mark (5)
4 Advance (7)
5 Trembling poplar (5)
6 Appropriate (5)
9 Authoress (anag.) (6,3)
14 Close companion (7)
15 Going away (7)
16 Flower shop (7)
19 Subject (5)
20 Acumen (5)
21 Group of eight (5)

210

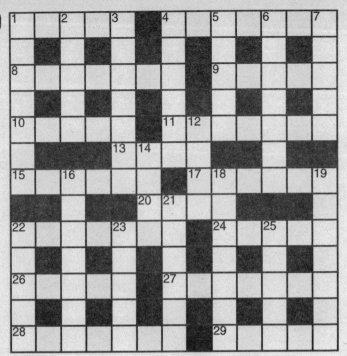

Across

1 Creator (5)
4 Plant in flower (7)
8 Spanish nobleman (7)
9 Useful (5)
10 A flavouring spice (5)
11 Work (7)
13 Of sound mind (4)
15 Push into (6)
17 Thoroughfare (6)
20 Wind instrument (4)
22 Greet on arrival (7)
24 Vicious claw (5)
26 Rub out (5)
27 Relative (7)
28 Small radio speaker (7)
29 Auburn haired (5)

Down

1 Foreign settler (7)
2 Military colour (5)
3 Compensation (7)
4 Resident of NW France (6)
5 yellowish brown pigment (5)
6 Commonplace (7)
7 Verse (5)
12 Mexican coin (4)
14 Small particle (4)
16 Let go (7)
18 Lockjaw (7)
19 Occupancy of building (7)
21 Flask (6)
22 Seize from another's grasp (5)
23 Public (5)
25 Citrus fruit (5)

Across

5 'Tom and ——' (cartoon) (5)
8 Small orange (8)
9 Digger (5)
10 Shell (8)
11 Perfect (5)
14 Dolt (3)
16 Summit (6)
17 Military display (6)
18 Cambs isle (3)
20 Adhere (5)
24 Outside (8)
25 Rascal (5)
26 Bestride (8)
27 Slope (5)

Down

1 Overgarment (5)
2 Grunt (5)
3 Lucky (5)
4 Zodiacal sign (6)
6 Hasten (8)
7 Heater (8)
12 Upright (8)
13 Farm worker (8)
14 Chopper (3)
15 Pig-pen (3)
19 Slackness (6)
21 Foot-lever (5)
22 Irish writer (5)
23 Salt and pepper (5)

212

Across

1 Companion (7)
5 Tows (5)
8 Set of maps (5)
9 Current indicator (7)
10 Meet (9)
12 Manage (3)
13 Vocalist (6)
14 Tried hard (6)
17 Fish-eggs (3)
18 Pressure gauge (9)
20 Eternal (7)
21 Consumed (5)
23 Weary (5)
24 Result (7)

Down

1 Stop (5)
2 Nothing (3)
3 Vague (7)
4 Characteristics (6)
5 Greek poet (5)
6 Extreme (9)
7 Odd (7)
11 Rival (9)
13 Snake (7)
15 Storm (7)
16 Wall-painting (6)
18 Mix (5)
19 Wash (5)
22 Pair (3)

Across

1 Chess pieces (7)
5 Loses heat (5)
8 Senior member of group (5)
9 Submarine missile (7)
10 Small brook (9)
12 Irritate (3)
13 Adjudge (6)
14 Bearing (6)
17 Ailing (3)
18 Drowsy (9)
20 River-bed cleaning vessel (7)
21 Endowment (5)
23 Supernumerary actor (5)
24 Frugality (7)

Down

1 Glory, prestige (5)
2 Very cold (3)
3 Report of Parliamentary proceedings (7)
4 Pay up (6)
5 Measure of purity of gold (5)
6 Acquiescence (9)
7 Game (7)
11 Remember (9)
13 Abate (7)
15 Tropical fruit (7)
16 Come into view (6)
18 Greek letter (5)
19 Spiced drink (5)
22 Fuss (3)

214

Across

1 Edible grain (6)
4 Religious procedures (5)
8 Distressed (5)
9 With rapidity (7)
10 Dead body (7)
11 Reticulated fabric (4)
12 Hostelry (3)
14 Hitler's deputy (4)
15 Gaelic (4)
18 Greek 't' (3)
21 Enthusiastic (4)
23 Make more taut (7)
25 Fascinate (7)
26 Loathe utterly (5)
27 Praise lavishly (5)
28 Miscellany (6)

Down

1 Place of worship (6)
2 Remains (7)
3 Vigorous party member (8)
4 Reckless (4)
5 Hackneyed (5)
6 Grass-cutter (6)
7 Shrill (5)
13 Yugoslav capital (8)
16 School bag (7)
17 Risky venture (6)
19 Unqualified (5)
20 Forcefulness (6)
22 Metal bar (5)
24 Resolution (4)

Across

1 Concur (5)
4 Fear (6)
9 Speak quietly (7)
10 Rely upon (5)
11 Pull vigorously (4)
12 Scent (7)
13 West-country river (3)
14 Flightless bird (4)
16 Large town (4)
18 Enquire (3)
20 Excess (7)
21 Spoken (4)
24 Ruffle (5)
25 Alligator pear (7)
26 Lake (6)
27 Country (5)

Down

1 Eternally (6)
2 Govern (5)
3 Glimpse (4)
5 Bowling feat (3-5)
6 Wine aroma (7)
7 Devotional song (6)
8 Fruit (5)
13 Final defeat (8)
15 Fish (7)
17 Handy (6)
18 Book of maps (5)
19 Nearly (6)
22 Prepared (5)
23 Italian city (4)

216

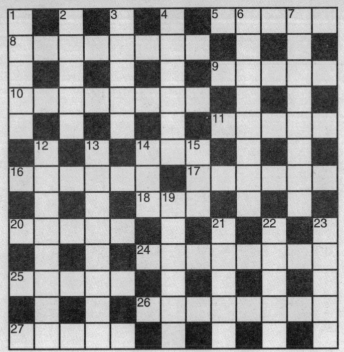

Across

5 Bathing beauty (5)
8 Squeezing out water (8)
9 Female dog (5)
10 Raw (8)
11 Dark beer (5)
14 Pig's pen (3)
16 Silvery metal (6)
17 Call up (6)
18 Cultural pursuits (3)
20 Unwanted paper (5)
24 Male horse (8)
25 Images (5)
26 Foot care (8)
27 Mealy mouthed person (5)

Down

1 Terrible (5)
2 Sorceress (5)
3 Snow house (5)
4 Sink money (6)
6 Compulsory vacation (8)
7 Expounded (8)
12 Upper arm joint (8)
13 Put together (8)
14 Stretch of water (3)
15 Still (3)
19 Bounder (6)
21 Threshing implement (5)
22 Infectious agent (5)
23 Go in (5)

217

Across

1 Sleepy state (6)
4 Dismissed (6)
7 Shapeless (9)
9 Playing-card (4)
10 Face-covering (4)
11 Pry (5)
13 Rampaged (6)
14 Steps (6)
15 Tumult (6)
17 Greatest height (6)
19 Bottom (5)
20 Enthralled (4)
22 Marijuana (4)
23 Forerunner (9)
24 Prickly sensation (6)
25 Attach (6)

Down

1 Projectile (6)
2 Unfeeling (4)
3 Short trip (6)
4 Teach (6)
5 Pal (4)
6 Stevedore (6)
7 Signature (9)
8 Wading bird (9)
11 Portable chair (5)
12 Father (5)
15 Eradicate (6)
16 Mob (6)
17 Garden flower (6)
18 Jumped (6)
21 Coarse seaweed (4)
22 Assistance (4)

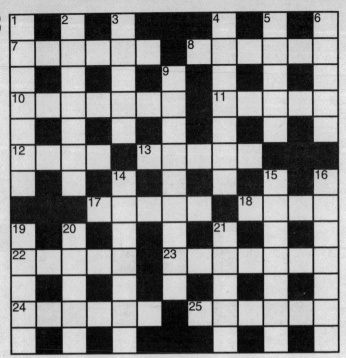

Across

7 Surge (6)
8 Gazes (6)
10 Exterior (7)
11 Play (5)
12 Watch (4)
13 Keyboard instrument (5)
17 Imbibe (5)
18 Visage (4)
22 Circular (5)
23 Nil (7)
24 Make (6)
25 Fair-haired (6)

Down

1 Pardon (7)
2 Dressed (7)
3 Reasoning (5)
4 Scholar (7)
5 wide (5)
6 Cinema award (5)
9 Start (9)
14 Learned (7)
15 Beaming (7)
16 Pretended (7)
19 Couple (5)
20 Silent (5)
21 Stem (5)

Across

1 Court of equity (8)
7 Blemishes (5)
8 Exaggerate (9)
9 Abyss (3)
10 Allow to fall (4)
11 Stinging insect (6)
13 Audacious (6)
14 Knitted garment (6)
17 False (6)
18 Way out (4)
20 Drinking-vessel (3)
22 Abode of recluses (9)
23 Foe (5)
24 Erudite (8)

Down

1 Multitude (5)
2 Wind-flower (7)
3 Barrel (4)
4 Sanity (6)
5 Vault (5)
6 Receptacle for smoker's residue (7)
7 Ramble (7)
12 Superficial, slight (7)
13 Insect (7)
15 Navigational instrument (7)
16 Rancid (6)
17 Capsize (5)
19 Thick cloth (5)
21 Metallic element (4)

220

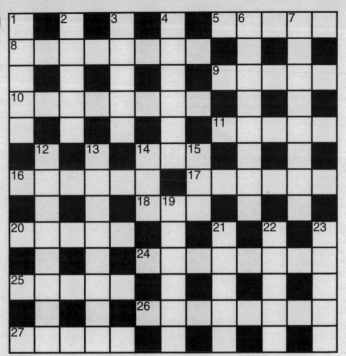

Across

5 Portion (5)
8 Pacts (8)
9 Employing (5)
10 Immodest (8)
11 Urge on (5)
14 Shed tears (3)
16 Mohair (6)
17 Bird house (6)
18 Chart (3)
20 Malediction (5)
24 Curved sword (8)
25 Bend down (5)
26 Charm (8)
27 Romany (5)

Down

1 Athenian (5)
2 South African grassland (5)
3 Soup base (5)
4 More enthusiastic (6)
6 Sleeplessness (8)
7 Australian capital (8)
12 Diligence (8)
13 Spicy semolina dish (8)
14 Rotating cylinder (3)
15 Sharp bark (3)
19 Esoteric (6)
21 Smug smile (5)
22 Retard growth (5)
23 Fish basket (5)

Across

1 Washes (6)
4 Shelter (5)
8 Large milk-can (5)
9 Weariness (7)
10 Model (7)
11 Retroussé (4)
12 Fresh (3)
14 Aquatic bird (4)
15 Glimpse (4)
18 Juice (3)
21 Reverberation (4)
23 Fisherman's bait (7)
25 Seasonal wind (7)
26 Entrails (5)
27 English poet (5)
28 Idolised (6)

Down

1 Periods of time (6)
2 Imitate (7)
3 Skittles (8)
4 Loathe (4)
5 Strict vegetarian (5)
6 Necessity (4-2)
7 Frequently (5)
13 Fine pottery (8)
16 Tender (7)
17 Homily (6)
19 Cheap wine (5)
20 Beamed (6)
22 Sweet substance (5)
24 Stud (4)

222

Across

1 Share dealer (6)
4 Container for liquid (6)
7 Blizzard (9)
9 Taunt (4)
10 Ancient Lebanese port (4)
11 Military practice (5)
13 Frank (6)
14 Church festival (6)
15 Repeat news (6)
17 Steal (6)
19 Mythological giant (5)
20 Eastern teacher (4)
22 Preliminary race (4)
23 Bound (9)
24 Famous physicist (6)
25 Unit of capacity (6)

Down

1 North European sea (6)
2 Southern county (4)
3 Recompense (6)
4 Military engagement (6)
5 Sour (4)
6 Make likeable (6)
7 Written name (9)
8 Puzzled (9)
11 Single number (5)
12 Classical language (5)
15 Type of coat (6)
16 Fungoid alga plant (6)
17 Upright board of fence (6)
18 Putrified (6)
21 The number one (4)
22 Cure (4)

223

Across

1 Per ardua ad —— (5)
4 Nothings (7)
8 Harmony (7)
9 Appetising (5)
10 Rash (5)
11 Leafage (7)
13 Cluster (4)
15 Froth (6)
17 Threaten (6)
20 Freshwater fish (4)
22 Detrimental (7)
24 Allowable (5)
26 Large animal (5)
27 Garden flower (7)
28 Notable (7)
29 Sign of omission (5)

Down

1 Intoxicant (7)
2 N African city (5)
3 Follower (7)
4 Fall asleep (3,3)
5 Before (5)
6 Prisoner (7)
7 Fashion (5)
12 Of the ear (4)
14 Pakistani language (4)
16 End-points (7)
18 Tuneful (7)
19 Take away (7)
21 Burning (6)
22 Throng (5)
23 Town in Somerset (5)
25 Supply food (5)

224

Across

1 Restrain (5)
4 Respiratory trouble (5)
10 Greed (7)
11 Natural aperient (5)
12 Loaded (5)
13 Flightless bird (7)
15 Colour (4)
17 Quick (5)
19 Command (5)
22 Run (4)
25 Type of dog (7)
27 Shelf (5)
29 Sponge (5)
30 Learner (7)
31 Kingdom (5)
32 Centre (5)

Down

2 Stockpile (5)
3 Italian wine (7)
5 Beginning (5)
6 Real (7)
7 Bird of prey (5)
8 Devil (5)
9 Sailing-boat (5)
14 Discontinue (4)
16 Inactive (4)
18 Shorten (7)
20 Set free (7)
21 Adhere (5)
23 Declaim (5)
24 At no time (5)
26 Perfect (5)
28 Giver (5)

Across

1 Tree (5)
4 Raised frame around ship's hatch (7)
8 Towards sheltered side (7)
9 Bird (5)
10 English. poet (5)
11 Syrupy medicine (7)
13 Encourage in crime (4)
15 Offspring before birth (6)
17 Wrinkle (6)
20 London district (4)
22 Unarmed self-defence system (7)
24 Bluish-purple (5)
26 IOW town (5)
27 Card-game (7)
28 Theatre gallery (7)
29 Took effect (5)

Down

1 Equilibrium (7)
2 Foe (5)
3 Rumour (7)
4 Pamper (6)
5 Gas (5)
6 Apathy (7)
7 Conjecture (5)
12 Irritation (4)
14 Chief (4)
16 Deck with gems (7)
18 European republic (7)
19 Precious stone (7)
21 Hullabaloo (6)
22 Twin of Esau (5)
23 Italian poet (5)
25 Perturbed (5)

226

Across

1 Water jug (7)
5 Combs (5)
8 Tibetan capital (5)
9 Non-jew (7)
10 Reckless (9)
12 Fitting (3)
13 Gaming establishment (6)
14 Heavenly signs (6)
17 Passenger vehicle (3)
18 Outward appearance (9)
20 Weather conditions (7)
21 Farewell (5)
23 Boredom (5)
24 Intrinsic nature (7)

Down

1 Eastern rice dish (5)
2 Beverage (3)
3 Pagan (7)
4 Esteem (6)
5 Astute (5)
6 Destruction (9)
7 Habitual doubter (7)
11 Preoccupation (9)
13 Sleeping compartment (7)
15 Northern French city (7)
16 Hinder (6)
18 Hindu teacher (5)
19 Musical study (5)
22 Hostelry (3)

Across

1 Express doubt (8)
7 Inheritors (5)
8 Costly (9)
9 Note on scale (3)
10 Come into view (4)
11 Go hungry (6)
13 Hurry (6)
14 Floor covering (6)
17 Add flavour (6)
18 Dry (4)
20 Insect (3)
22 A rusty can (anag.) (9)
23 Hindu princess (5)
24 Italian cheese (8)

Down

1 Suppress (5)
2 Hires (7)
3 Lilliputian (4)
4 Narcotic drug (6)
5 Fine cotton fabric (5)
6 Bituminous substance (7)
7 Rumour (7)
12 Since (7)
13 German city (7)
15 Possibly (7)
16 Part of the eye (6)
17 French river (5)
19 Senior member (5)
21 Staunch (4)

228

Across

1 Thickened gravy (5)
4 Mistake (5)
10 Guard (7)
11 Wild pea (5)
12 Antique novelty (5)
13 Strip of bacon fat (7)
15 Exposed (4)
17 Wind instrument (5)
19 Belief (5)
22 Tip (4)
25 Finger guard (7)
27 Brief (5)
29 Measure (5)
30 Untidy mess (7)
31 Insignificant (5)
32 Facial hair (5)

Down

2 Love affair (5)
3 Thin cigar (7)
5 Wanderer (5)
6 Result (7)
7 Flavouring agent (5)
8 Not fresh (5)
9 Cogitate (5)
14 Gambling stake (4)
16 Ringing of bells (4)
18 Spare time (7)
20 Squeeze out (7)
21 Theatrical platform (5)
23 Fruit (5)
24 River boat (5)
26 Cry like a lamb (5)
28 Helicopter propeller (5)

Across

1 Pepper (6)
4 Origin (6)
7 Four-legged animal (9)
9 Trip (4)
10 Queen of Carthage (4)
11 Small cut (5)
13 Unmarried (6)
14 Performs (6)
15 Disgust (6)
17 Tray (6)
19 Tartan cloth (5)
20 Slipper (4)
22 Operatic song (4)
23 Furthest point (9)
24 Saying (6)
25 Whisper (6)

Down

1 Desert plant (6)
2 Scowl (4)
3 Halogen element (6)
4 Floodgate (6)
5 Exploited (4)
6 Mould in relief (6)
7 Fivefold (9)
8 Exploration (9)
11 Snooze (5)
12 Work dough (5)
15 Great hunter (6)
16 Warning sound (6)
17 Boil gently (6)
18 Harvester (6)
21 Way out (4)
22 Minute particle (4)

230

Across

1 Limp (4)
3 Scottish cattle (8)
9 Name (5)
10 Calumnious (7)
11 Flow (3)
13 Disinclined (9)
14 Young swan (6)
16 Relax (6)
18 Rigidity (9)
20 Obtain (3)
22 Maintained (7)
23 Cereal (5)
25 Hated (8)
26 Lake (4)

Down

1 Subsequently (5)
2 Mesh (3)
4 Annually (6)
5 Slight amount (7)
6 Copying (9)
7 Chosen (7)
8 Expensive (4)
12 Remiss (9)
14 Sweet sauce (7)
15 Attempts (7)
17 Interfere (6)
19 Indication (4)
21 Strained (5)
24 Beer (3)

Across

5 —— Garbo (5)
8 Act of drawing or pulling (8)
9 Expert (5)
10 Esoteric (8)
11 Aquatic creature (5)
14 Filthy place (3)
16 Bone in leg (6)
17 Become famous (6)
18 Immerse (3)
20 Field of play (5)
24 Acclaim (8)
25 Molten rock (5)
26 Glue (8)
27 Wading bird (5)

Down

1 Slink (5)
2 Spurious (5)
3 Forbidding (5)
4 Pamper (6)
6 Songbird (8)
7 Having high centre of gravity (3-5)
12 Watchful (8)
13 Tuned percussion instrument (8)
14 Doleful (3)
15 Yelp (3)
19 Hinder (6)
21 Swift (5)
22 Ghastly (5)
23 Postpone (5)

232

Across

1 Pugilist (7)
5 Unadorned (5)
8 Emblem of office (5)
9 Of the heart (7)
10 Uplift (7)
11 Hunting weapon (5)
12 Good-luck charm (6)
14 Gaseous element (6)
17 Hazardous (5)
19 Tidy (7)
22 Loss of memory (7)
23 Nebraskan city (5)
24 Friendship (5)
25 Put into words (7)

Down

1 Moral tale (5)
2 Impious (7)
3 Greek letter (5)
4 Loud commotion (6)
5 Bewilder (7)
6 Foreigner (5)
7 Atomic particle (7)
12 Sweet, fortified wine (7)
13 Homeric poem (7)
15 Domestic waste (7)
16 Fealty (6)
18 Egyptian peninsula (5)
20 Flag (5)
21 Irish poet (5)

Across

5 Athletic pastime (5)
8 Rebellious act (8)
9 Veracity (5)
10 Cosmetic (8)
11 Young bird (5)
14 Curve (3)
16 Material (6)
17 Outcome (6)
18 Plaything (3)
20 Elevate (5)
24 Nearby (8)
25 Woo (5)
26 Party set (anag.) (8)
27 Underworld (5)

Down

1 Sacred song (5)
2 Skilful (5)
3 Declare (5)
4 Agree (6)
6 Buy (8)
7 Small bag (8)
12 Amorous adventurer (8)
13 Protect (8)
14 Perform (3)
15 Weep (3)
19 Out-of-date (3-3)
21 Tag (5)
22 Pier (5)
23 Corset (5)

234

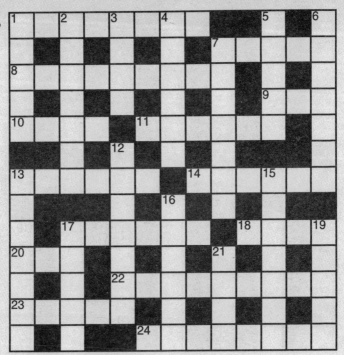

Across

1 Supported by water (8)
7 On one's own (5)
8 Passing (9)
9 Male offspring (3)
10 Nazi greeting (4)
11 Calm and dignified (6)
13 Discuss (6)
14 Arachnid (6)
17 Choosing (6)
18 Retired for the night (4)
20 Animal foot (3)
22 True to life (9)
23 Remove errors from (5)
24 Put off (8)

Down

1 Go and bring (5)
2 Applause (7)
3 Russian news agency (4)
4 Female relatives (6)
5 Signal code (5)
6 Wander (7)
7 Try (7)
12 Gymnastic costume (7)
13 Mental hand-up (7)
15 One who argues a case (7)
16 Employ (6)
17 Possessed (5)
19 Gambled (5)
21 Plunge into water (4)

Across

1 Direct (8)
7 Intertwined (5)
8 Avenue (9)
9 Young demon (3)
10 Feeble (4)
11 Wagered (6)
13 Beer and lemonade (6)
14 Concurred (6)
17 Wall-painting (6)
18 Wither (4)
20 Spoil (3)
22 Easily shocked (9)
23 Ooze (5)
24 Carriage (8)

Down

1 Sharpen (5)
2 Circular building (7)
3 Lazily (4)
4 Fitness (6)
5 Pungent (5)
6 Adjusted (7)
7 Disclosure (7)
12 Contrary (7)
13 Conjecture (7)
15 Volume (7)
16 Real (6)
17 Delicate (5)
19 Laugh (5)
21 Equitable (4)

236

Across

1 Coast (5)
4 Sufficient (6)
9 Underground stem (7)
10 Ire (5)
11 Identical (4)
12 Run of luck (7)
13 Non-clerical (3)
14 Wise men (4)
16 Leguminous plant (4)
18 Idiot (3)
20 Glassy coatings (7)
21 Be scared of (4)
24 Corpulent (5)
25 Torment (7)
26 Fastidious stylist (6)
27 Crave (5)

Down

1 Emphasis (6)
2 Hatred (5)
3 God of love (4)
5 Proximity (8)
6 Exigency (7)
7 Book on plants (6)
8 Racing classic (5)
13 Inanimate (8)
15 Non-professional (7)
17 Reimburse (6)
18 Egyptian dam (5)
19 Parentless child (6)
22 Heath (5)
23 Unsightly (4)

Across

7 Refuse to work (6)
8 Agreement (6)
10 Revel noisily (7)
11 Coral ring (5)
12 Stupid fellow (4)
13 Horse (5)
17 Strict and serious (5)
18 Cleanse (4)
22 Light beam (5)
23 Nuclear weapon (7)
24 Fit for ploughing (6)
25 Boy friend (6)

Down

1 With feet apart (7)
2 Blind print (7)
3 Slide over ice (5)
4 Abraded (7)
5 One of low intelligence (5)
6 Fully grown (5)
9 Verbal tense (9)
14 Frighten (7)
15 Very hot spice (7)
16 Idle talk (7)
19 Cry like a lamb (5)
20 Film award (5)
21 Fairy like being (5)

238

Across

1 Most succinct (8)
7 Underground stems (5)
8 Meddle (9)
9 Tibetan gazelle (3)
10 Hard wood (4)
11 Fine clothes (6)
13 Military rebellion (6)
14 Cherry-red (6)
17 Thunderstruck (6)
18 Incentive (4)
20 Drunkard (3)
22 Iniquitous (9)
23 Gentleman's attendant (5)
24 Immaculate (8)

Down

1 Relay of workers (5)
2 Pariah (7)
3 Mountain lake (4)
4 Scabbard (6)
5 Blacksmith's shop (5)
6 Runaway prisoner (7)
7 Well-bred (7)
12 Captivate (7)
13 Official letter (7)
15 Entreat (7)
16 Functional (6)
17 Coral island (5)
19 Hazards (5)
21 Tie (4)

Across

1 Captured (6)
4 Get up (5)
8 Accumulate (5)
9 Set free (7)
10 Most serious (7)
11 Yield (4)
12 Very warm (3)
14 Lake (4)
15 Above (4)
18 Noise (3)
21 Job (4)
23 Voter (7)
25 Copy (7)
26 In front (5)
27 Go in (5)
28 Water-heater (6)

Down

1 Alter (6)
2 Ignorant (7)
3 Rushed (8)
4 Confederate (4)
5 Stupid (5)
6 Football team (6)
7 Soup (5)
13 Put up with (8)
16 Beg (7)
17 Try hard (6)
19 At no time (5)
20 Card-game (6)
22 Rapid (5)
24 Equitable (4)

240

Across

1 Betray to police (5)
4 Courses for journeys (6)
9 Down-to-earth philosophy (7)
10 Slight colour (5)
11 Vein of ore (4)
12 Whip for punishment (7)
13 Beast of burden (3)
14 Poet (4)
16 A number (4)
18 100 square metres (3)
20 Formal agreement (7)
21 Implement (4)
24 Line of mountains (5)
25 Very old (7)
26 Corrections (6)
27 US stock farm (5)

Down

1 Wash out throat (6)
2 Grant (5)
3 Set of clothes (4)
5 Detached building (8)
6 Fit of temper (7)
7 Jewish coin (6)
8 Heap together (5)
13 Standing next to (8)
15 Hospital social worker (7)
17 In short supply (6)
18 Book of maps (5)
19 Grasp (6)
22 Great sea (5)
23 Maple genus (4)

The Answers

1 _____

ACROSS:1 Chopping, **7** Etude, **8** Overdraft, **9** Spa, **10** Nail, **11** Active, **13** Digest, **14** Baffle, **17** Isaiah, **18** Crop, **20** Run, **22** Intricate, **23** Cynic, **24** Pantheon.
DOWN: 1 Clown, **2** Opening, **3** Pads, **4** Nuance, **5** Curse, **6** Debacle, **7** Ethical, **12** Islamic, **13** Derrick, **15** Forsake, **16** Mantra, **17** Inane, **19** Paean, **21** Rift.

2 _____

ACROSS:7 Scorch, **8** Dearth, **10** Long ago, **11** Expel, **12** Each, **13** Aspen, **17** Broad, **18** Trio, **22** Egret, **23** Croquet, **24** Supper, **25** Dollar.
DOWN: 1 Psalter, **2** Connect, **3** Scrap, **4** Jezebel, **5** Tripe, **6** Whelk, **9** Constance, **14** Pretzel, **15** Trouble, **16** Posture, **19** Beast, **20** Grape, **21** Motor.

3 _____

ACROSS:1 Church, **4** Belle, **8** Ariel, **9** Compact, **10** Trouble, **11** Beer, **12** Wig, **14** Amps, **15** Riga, **18** Hog, **21** Ramp, **23** Referee, **25** Confess, **26** Infer, **27** Dirty, **28** Direct.
DOWN: 1 Crafty, **2** Uniform, **3** Calabash, **4** Bomb, **5** Lease, **6** Extort, **7** Screw, **13** Graffiti, **16** Giraffe, **17** Braced, **19** Gross, **20** Ferret, **22** Miner, **24** Lely.

4 _____

ACROSS:1 Straiten, **7** Arrow, **8** Universal, **9** Sot, **10** Dawn, **11** Egress, **13** Mayfly, **14** Uglier, **17** Fitter, **18** Plus, **20** Tar, **22** Heartless, **23** Funny, **24** Proposal.
DOWN: 1 Squad, **2** Railway, **3** Idea, **4** Ensign, **5** Gross, **6** Twitter, **7** Allergy, **12** Blotchy, **13** Mastiff, **15** Illness, **16** Repair, **17** Front, **19** Sisal, **21** Step.

5 _____

ACROSS:1 Missed, **4** Aches, **8** Moose, **9** Onerous, **10** Nothing, **11** Shoe, **12** Hit, **14** Inch, **15** Alto, **18** Two, **21** Plan, **23** Furrier, **25** Cottage, **26** Genre, **27** Early, **28** Energy.
DOWN: 1 Moment, **2** Shorten, **3** Eyesight, **4** Apex, **5** Hooch, **6** Sister, **7** Bough, **13** Tarragon, **16** Thinner, **17** Apache, **19** Offer, **20** Greedy, **22** After, **24** Wary.

6 _____

ACROSS:1 Scent, **4** Appease, **8** Endless, **9** Sward, **10** Towel, **11** Meander, **13** Item, **15** Refuse, **17** Magnum, **20** Road, **22** Parvenu, **24** Valet, **26** Leith, **27** Largess, **28** Aircrew, **29** Ensue.
DOWN: 1 Shelter, **2** Endow, **3** Trellis, **4** Assume, **5** Pasta, **6** Aladdin, **7** Elder, **12** Emma, **14** Tern, **16** Farrier, **18** Adverse, **19** Matisse, **21** Outlaw, **22** Polka, **23** Ether, **25** Leeds.

7 _____

ACROSS:1 Eiffel, **4** Asleep, **7** Monastery, **9** Plod, **10** Dock, **11** Gnome, **13** Despot, **14** Napkin, **15** Tirade, **17** Lethal, **19** Steer, **20** Lout, **22** Drag, **23** Signature, **24** Rustic, **25** Remedy.
DOWN: 1 Eloped, **2** Food, **3** Learnt, **4** Autumn, **5** Lord, **6** Parkin, **7** Monstrous, **8** Yorkshire, **11** Goods, **12** Eager, **15** Tiller, **16** Ethnic, **17** Letter, **18** Legacy, **21** Tint, **22** Drum.

8 _____

ACROSS:1 Fizzy, **4** Calais, **9** Cabbage, **10** Nacre, **11** Drag, **12** Mislaid, **13** May, **14** Pine, **16** Inca, **18** Roc, **20** Outline, **21** Bath, **24** Lyric, **25** Emulate, **26** Damsel, **27** Tress.
DOWN: 1 Facade, **2** Zebra, **3** Year, **5** Agnostic, **6** Archaic, **7** Speedy, **8** Jemmy, **13** Mediocre, **15** Interim, **17** Toiled, **18** Refer, **19** Cheers, **22** Awake, **23** Punt.

9 _____

ACROSS:1 Forte, **4** Thieves, **8** Twitter, **9** Inner, **10** Obese, **11** Similar, **13** Acts, **15** Siesta, **17** Levant, **20** Step, **22** Trieste, **24** Satin, **26** Alien, **27** Pulsate, **28** Treacle, **29** Night.
DOWN: 1 Fatuous, **2** Rhine, **3** Entreat, **4** Thrust, **5** Idiom, **6** Vanilla, **7** Surer, **12** Isle, **14** Cast, **16** Edifice, **18** Epsilon, **19** Tangent, **21** Temple, **22** Trait, **23** Sonic, **25** Twang.

10 _____

ACROSS:1 Cooker, **4** Burrow, **7** Slowcoach, **9** Thin, **10** Kerb, **11** Frock, **13** Hunted, **14** Honest, **15** Ostend, **17** Manful, **19** Texan, **20** Ezra, **22** Fern, **23** Endeavour, **24** Outwit, **25** Ladder.
DOWN: 1 Clutch, **2** Kiln, **3** Reward, **4** Brooch, **5** Rack, **6** Wombat, **7** Signature, **8** Hereafter, **11** Feint, **12** Koran, **15** Overdo, **16** Defect, **17** Marvel, **18** Lancer, **21** Anew, **22** Fund.

11 ————

ACROSS:**1** Stare, **4** Allies, **9** Martini, **10** Yield, **11** Reef, **12** Habitat, **13** Set, **14** Adit, **16** Utah, **18** Get, **20** Outrage, **21** Open, **24** Swing, **25** Swallow, **26** Lustre, **27** Tutor.
DOWN: **1** Sombre, **2** Agree, **3** Evil, **5** Layabout, **6** Inertia, **7** Sedate, **8** Sight, **13** Stranger, **15** Ditties, **17** Morsel, **18** Geese, **19** Answer, **22** Pilot, **23** Pact.

12 ————

ACROSS:**1** Advent, **4** Chores, **7** Esperanto, **9** Eddy, **10** Smug, **11** Otter, **13** Salary, **14** Tumult, **15** Ocelot, **17** Reason, **19** Poker, **20** Task, **22** Pail, **23** Simpleton, **24** Thrive, **25** Titian.
DOWN: **1** Access, **2** Easy, **3** Treaty, **4** Chalet, **5** Oats, **6** Slight, **7** Edelweiss, **8** Ombudsman, **11** Orlop, **12** Ruler, **15** Outwit, **16** Topple, **17** Recent, **18** Nelson, **21** Kiwi, **22** Post.

13 ————

ACROSS:**1** Chips, **4** Steward, **8** Onerous, **9** Haver, **10** Sated, **11** Essence, **13** Earn, **15** Stride, **17** Upkeep, **20** Orgy, **22** Decline, **24** Jolly, **26** Equal, **27** Immense, **28** Spectre, **29** Sadat.
DOWN: **1** Croesus, **2** Inert, **3** Scolded, **4** Sister, **5** Ethos, **6** Advance, **7** Dirge, **12** Snug, **14** Aeon, **16** Recluse, **18** Pyjamas, **19** Payment, **21** Refine, **22** Dregs, **23** Inlet, **25** Lined.

14 ————

ACROSS:**1** Fowl, **3** Language, **9** Ounce, **10** Princes, **11** Kit, **13** Precursor, **14** Weasel, **16** Debris, **18** Desperado, **20** Leo, **22** Isolate, **23** Equal, **25** Gelatine, **26** Feed.
DOWN: **1** Flock, **2** Win, **4** Apples, **5** Guipure, **6** Ancestral, **7** Ensures, **8** Leap, **12** Toadstool, **14** Wadding, **15** Elegant, **17** Tavern, **19** Over, **21** Oiled, **24** Use.

15 ————

ACROSS:**1** Crank, **4** Handel, **9** Scarlet, **10** Disco, **11** Lady, **12** Declare, **13** Buy, **14** Urge, **16** Tidy, **18** Fee, **20** Admiral, **21** Able, **24** Quick, **25** Trebled, **26** Engine, **27** Layer.
DOWN: **1** Castle, **2** Award, **3** Kilt, **5** Abdicate, **6** Discard, **7** Looted, **8** Study, **13** Bearskin, **15** Romping, **17** Barque, **18** Flute, **19** Leader, **22** Bully, **23** Well.

16 ————

ACROSS:**1** Sought, **4** Threw, **8** Carob, **9** Cubicle, **10** Regatta, **11** Oyez, **12** Gem, **14** Stoa, **15** Iamb, **18** Lad, **21** Hold, **23** Adjourn, **25** Villain, **26** Dante, **27** Rheum, **28** Beadle.
DOWN: **1** Secure, **2** Upright, **3** Habitual, **4** Tuba, **5** Rocky, **6** Wheeze, **7** Scrag, **13** Misjudge, **16** Mourned, **17** Shaver, **19** Daunt, **20** Sneeze, **22** Lille, **24** Calm.

17 ————

ACROSS:**1** Welling, **5** Tonne, **8** Erase, **9** Article, **10** Talkative, **12** Ape, **13** Easter, **14** Assist, **17** Ski, **18** Senseless, **20** Launder, **21** Terse, **23** Niece, **24** Endless.
DOWN: **1** Wheat, **2** Lea, **3** Iterate, **4** Gratis, **5** Title, **6** Nectarine, **7** Everest, **11** Lassitude, **13** Epsilon, **15** Scented, **16** Untrue, **18** Sedge, **19** Steps, **22** Roe.

18 ————

ACROSS:**1** Promise, **5** Skuas, **8** Nudge, **9** Cruiser, **10** Carotid, **11** Total, **12** Scythe, **14** Aramis, **17** Bloom, **19** Endemic, **22** Regards, **23** Ashen, **24** Sinus, **25** Stetson.
DOWN: **1** Panic, **2** Orderly, **3** Inert, **4** Escudo, **5** Saunter, **6** Upset, **7** Surplus, **12** Suburbs, **13** Humerus, **15** Memphis, **16** Versus, **18** Organ, **20** Drape, **21** Canon.

19 ————

ACROSS:**1** Grass, **4** Routes, **9** Martial, **10** Padre, **11** Odds, **12** Candour, **13** Irk, **14** Clan, **16** Nosy, **18** Fit, **20** Sincere, **21** Feat, **24** Etude, **25** Salsify, **26** Pirate, **27** Sated.
DOWN: **1** Gambol, **2** Acrid, **3** Skin, **5** Opponent, **6** Tedious, **7** Sierra, **8** Flock, **13** Indecent, **15** Languor, **17** Asleep, **18** Feast, **19** Stayed, **22** Eliot, **23** Alms.

20 ————

ACROSS:**5** Razor, **8** Question, **9** Avoid, **10** Implicit, **11** Scent, **14** Men, **16** Banana, **17** Outlaw, **18** Dew, **20** Leapt, **24** December, **25** Plain, **26** Aperture, **27** Lager.
DOWN: **1** Squid, **2** Tempo, **3** Strip, **4** Polite, **6** Advocate, **7** Oriental, **12** Camellia, **13** Sapphire, **14** Mad, **15** Now, **19** Exempt, **21** Metre, **22** About, **23** Ariel.

21 ————
ACROSS:**7** Waiter, **8** Little, **10** Syringe, **11** Olive, **12** Mate, **13** Strew, **17** Barmy, **18** Keel, **22** Extra, **23** Narrate, **24** Cancer, **25** Effete.
DOWN: **1** Twosome, **2** Migrate, **3** Seine, **4** Widower, **5** Staid, **6** Melee, **9** Sentiment, **14** Manager, **15** Relaxed, **16** Fleeced, **19** Fence, **20** Stone, **21** Craft.

22 ————
ACROSS:**1** Chain, **4** Berlin, **9** Natural, **10** Tibet, **11** Race, **12** Mongrel, **13** Rob, **14** Bath, **16** Lull, **18** Pie, **20** Recital, **21** Able, **24** Their, **25** Tableau, **26** Detect, **27** Event.
DOWN: **1** Canary, **2** Aztec, **3** Norm, **5** Entangle, **6** Liberal, **7** Nettle, **8** Plumb, **13** Rhetoric, **15** Ancient, **17** Grated, **18** Pluto, **19** Result, **22** Breve, **23** Oboe.

23 ————
ACROSS:**7** Setter, **8** Sighed, **10** Overdue, **11** Piece, **12** Nice, **13** Usual, **17** Point, **18** Love, **22** Peril, **23** Example, **24** Naples, **25** Forest.
DOWN: **1** Astound, **2** Stretch, **3** Needy, **4** Display, **5** Cheer, **6** Adder, **9** Personnel, **14** Collier, **15** Complex, **16** Beneath, **19** Spine, **20** Erupt, **21** Canoe.

24 ————
ACROSS:**5** Chest, **8** Ornament, **9** Clear, **10** Recorder, **11** Fresh, **14** Odd, **16** Frugal, **17** Option, **18** Dig, **20** Aglow, **24** Windpipe, **25** Pagan, **26** Slagheap, **27** State.
DOWN: **1** Hoard, **2** Knack, **3** Smirk, **4** Intend, **6** Hilarity, **7** Snapshot, **12** Fragrant, **13** Ignorant, **14** Old, **15** Dog, **19** Icicle, **21** Adage, **22** Bizet, **23** Tempt.

25 ————
ACROSS:**1** Gray, **3** Eminence, **9** Obese, **10** Haricot, **11** Sop, **13** Eliminate, **14** Deride, **16** Thrift, **18** Sheltered, **20** Ego, **22** Elegist, **23** Lunch, **25** Dressing, **26** Glee.
DOWN: **1** Gloss, **2** Aye, **4** Mohair, **5** Norwich, **6** Nectarine, **7** Entreat, **8** Fete, **12** Persevere, **14** Distend, **15** Details, **17** Breton, **19** Dale, **21** Ochre, **24** Nil.

26 ————
ACROSS:**1** Think, **4** Allowed, **8** Biscuit, **9** Monet, **10** Steak, **11** October, **13** Lure, **15** Oyster, **17** Naught, **20** Gate, **22** Smother, **24** Rivet, **26** Expel, **27** Insulin, **28** Project, **29** Lotus.
DOWN: **1** Tabasco, **2** Issue, **3** Knuckle, **4** Author, **5** Limit, **6** Windbag, **7** Deter, **12** Cent, **14** Urge, **16** Scorpio, **18** Aerosol, **19** Tetanus, **21** Artist, **22** Sheep, **23** Halve, **25** Valet.

27 ————
ACROSS:**5** Grate, **8** Unwashed, **9** Scone, **10** Reliable, **11** Freed, **14** Era, **16** Malign, **17** Peeler, **18** Doe, **20** Grout, **24** Stumbled, **25** Ideal, **26** Anathema, **27** Creek.
DOWN: **1** Curry, **2** Twill, **3** Oscar, **4** Dealer, **6** Recorder, **7** Tendered, **12** Labrador, **13** Simulate, **14** End, **15** Ape, **19** Outing, **21** Smith, **22** Sleep, **23** Ideas.

28 ————
ACROSS:**1** Orion, **4** Tiering, **8** Tidings, **9** Binge, **10** Pixie, **11** Low-down, **13** Reef, **15** Selwyn, **17** Fiesta, **20** Veal, **22** Synonym, **24** Lhasa, **26** Preen, **27** Organic, **28** Lengthy, **29** Limbo.
DOWN: **1** Octopus, **2** Index, **3** Nunnery, **4** Tussle, **5** Elbow, **6** Igneous, **7** Glean, **12** Offa, **14** Envy, **16** Lantern, **18** Illegal, **19** Ajaccio, **21** Embody, **22** Sepal, **23** Nonet, **25** Annam.

29 ————
ACROSS:**1** Choir, **4** Chewed, **9** Prelate, **10** Sorry, **11** Erne, **12** Outsize, **13** Fan, **14** Able, **16** Torn, **18** Foe, **20** Reserve, **21** Stop, **24** Piano, **25** Gourmet, **26** Redden, **27** Paddy.
DOWN: **1** Copper, **2** Ocean, **3** Rear, **5** Hesitate, **6** Warrior, **7** Dryden, **8** Felon, **13** Fearsome, **15** Bustard, **17** Proper, **18** Feign, **19** Apathy, **22** Timid, **23** Jump.

30 ————
ACROSS:**1** Knoll, **4** Legible, **8** Sustain, **9** Green, **10** Rates, **11** Eclipse, **13** Oath, **15** Lomond, **17** Affray, **20** Zero, **22** Perplex, **24** Reads, **26** Songs, **27** Theorem, **28** Erratic, **29** Track.
DOWN: **1** Kestrel, **2** Onset, **3** Liaison, **4** Lancet, **5** Gogol, **6** Bleeper, **7** Ernie, **12** Char, **14** Adze, **16** Mariner, **18** Forfeit, **19** Yashmak, **21** Exotic, **22** Paste, **23** Liszt, **25** Aorta.

31 ———

ACROSS:**1** Grease, **4** Proof, **8** Value, **9** Laconic, **10** Revelry, **11** Arid, **12** Duo, **14** Anon, **15** Site, **18** Gum, **21** Tomb, **23** Abusive, **25** Artless, **26** Asked, **27** Troop, **28** Sentry.
DOWN: **1** Govern, **2** Enliven, **3** Sterling, **4** Pact, **5** Owner, **6** Facade, **7** Clwyd, **13** Osculate, **16** Thicket, **17** Stuart, **19** Manse, **20** Deadly, **22** Metro, **24** Kelp.

32 ———

ACROSS:**7** Coster, **8** Counts, **10** Primula, **11** Pinto, **12** Laid, **13** Green, **17** Mecca, **18** Seer, **22** Hazel, **23** Diamond, **24** Spruce, **25** Cognac.
DOWN: **1** Scapula, **2** Aspirin, **3** Debut, **4** Complex, **5** Inane, **6** Ascot, **9** Matricide, **14** Fetlock, **15** Resound, **16** Predict, **19** Those, **20** Azure, **21** Havoc.

33 ———

ACROSS:**1** Muster, **4** Weigh, **8** Roost, **9** Haggard, **10** Largess, **11** Byre, **12** Top, **14** Gnat, **15** Rapt, **18** Yen, **21** Tomb, **23** Assured, **25** Ballade, **26** Inept, **27** Error, **28** Welded.
DOWN: **1** Morale, **2** Sporran, **3** Entreaty, **4** Wage, **5** Italy, **6** Hedged, **7** Whist, **13** Prestige, **16** Portend, **17** Stable, **19** Naked, **20** Edited, **22** Molar, **24** Lair.

34 ———

ACROSS:**1** Boulder, **5** Noble, **8** Green, **9** Brittle, **10** Serviette, **12** Aga, **13** Coyote, **14** Finish, **17** Raj, **18** Goldfinch, **20** Obviate, **21** Renew, **23** Naked, **24** Trooper.
DOWN: **1** Bogus, **2** Use, **3** Dentist, **4** Rebate, **5** Noise, **6** Battalion, **7** Eyewash, **11** Reykjavik, **13** Cartoon, **15** Inferno, **16** Client, **18** Grand, **19** Hewer, **22** Nap.

35 ———

ACROSS:**1** Brays, **4** Knows, **10** Conceal, **11** Verse, **12** Amend, **13** Narrate, **15** Edge, **17** Spade, **19** Ovate, **22** Erne, **25** Warfare, **27** Round, **29** Meter, **30** Leisure, **31** Ashen, **32** Stalk.
DOWN: **2** Rinse, **3** Yielded, **5** Never, **6** Warrant, **7** Scrap, **8** Cling, **9** Rebel, **14** Aeon, **16** Deer, **18** Pirates, **20** Verdict, **21** Swamp, **23** Realm, **24** Adder, **26** Agree, **28** Usual.

36 ———

ACROSS:**1** Scent, **4** Tralee, **9** Radical, **10** Tithe, **11** Work, **12** Profuse, **13** Woe, **14** Pale, **16** Aver, **18** Col, **20** Regular, **21** Step, **24** Cello, **25** Spanner, **26** Sector, **27** Niche.
DOWN: **1** Scrawl, **2** Elder, **3** Tact, **5** Rational, **6** Lettuce, **7** Exeter, **8** Slope, **13** Well-to-do, **15** Angelic, **17** Crocus, **18** Crash, **19** Sparse, **22** Tonic, **23** Barn.

37 ———

ACROSS:**5** Share, **8** Prophets, **9** Ideal, **10** Elongate, **11** Unite, **14** Lea, **16** Tuxedo, **17** Custom, **18** Tee, **20** Chaos, **24** Criminal, **25** Frail, **26** Enormous, **27** Pasha.
DOWN: **1** Upset, **2** Donor, **3** Whigs, **4** Statue, **6** Hedonist, **7** Reaction, **12** Euphoria, **13** Demolish, **14** Lot, **15** Ace, **19** Erring, **21** Smart, **22** Annoy, **23** Blush.

38 ———

ACROSS:**1** Expert, **4** Tease, **8** Holes, **9** Termite, **10** Laconic, **11** Ugli, **12** Kos, **14** Anon, **15** Ahem, **18** Tea, **21** Risk, **23** Caviare, **25** Chatter, **26** Grime, **27** Satin, **28** Aspect.
DOWN: **1** Exhale, **2** Pelican, **3** Resonant, **4** Tart, **5** Aping, **6** Eyelid, **7** Stack, **13** Salvages, **16** Examine, **17** Crocus, **19** Acorn, **20** Select, **22** Smart, **24** Eton.

39 ———

ACROSS:**1** Watcher, **5** Doone, **8** Loess, **9** Pungent, **10** Sincerity, **12** Hoe, **13** Access, **14** Cobalt, **17** Ass, **18** Processor, **20** Arabian, **21** Assay, **23** Thyme, **24** Thermal.
DOWN: **1** Wales, **2** Tie, **3** Hostess, **4** Repair, **5** Dandy, **6** Overheads, **7** Entreat, **11** Necessary, **13** Adamant, **15** Operate, **16** Bonnet, **18** Price, **19** Royal, **22** Sum.

40 ———

ACROSS:**1** Part, **3** Ticklers, **9** Repel, **10** Monster, **11** Hop, **13** Detective, **14** Choppy, **16** Sprain, **18** Promenade, **20** Eat, **22** Trivial, **23** Cower, **25** Landmark, **26** Oxen.
DOWN: **1** Parch, **2** Rip, **4** Inmate, **5** Kingcup, **6** Extricate, **7** Surgeon, **8** Clad, **12** Promotion, **14** Capital, **15** Premium, **17** Sailor, **19** Each, **21** Turin, **24** Wax.

41 —————

ACROSS:1 Wrecked, 5 Oriel, 8 Spume, 9 Beastly, 10 Selective, 12 Rot, 13 Canape, 14 Delete, 17 Ass, 18 Confident, 20 Leafage, 21 Tenor, 23 Scent, 24 Theatre.

DOWN: 1 Wasps, 2 Emu, 3 Kneecap, 4 Debris, 5 Ovate, 6 Interfere, 7 Layette, 11 Landscape, 13 Chablis, 15 Epistle, 16 Insert, 18 Chart, 19 Three, 22 Net.

42 —————

ACROSS:5 Bawls, 8 Sapphire, 9 Spade, 10 Lollipop, 11 Grebe, 14 Wet, 16 Radish, 17 Ignore, 18 Yap, 20 Pilot, 24 Revolver, 25 Giddy, 26 Fugitive, 27 Inert.

DOWN: 1 Psalm, 2 Apple, 3 Chair, 4 Groove, 6 Apparent, 7 Ladybird, 12 Magician, 13 Disorder, 14 Why, 15 Tip, 19 Avenue, 21 Topic, 22 Avoid, 23 Greed.

43 —————

ACROSS:1 Black, 4 Bored, 10 Grouser, 11 Erect, 12 Piece, 13 Lenient, 15 Wilt, 17 Boast, 19 Omits, 22 Cone, 25 Delight, 27 Loser, 29 Rogue, 30 Endless, 31 Edits, 32 Score.

DOWN: 2 Loose, 3 Cashews, 5 Ocean, 6 Element, 7 Agape, 8 Drill, 9 State, 14 Eton, 16 Itch, 18 Obliged, 20 Melodic, 21 Adore, 23 Otter, 24 Brass, 26 Great, 28 Swear.

44 —————

ACROSS:1 Poster, 4 Broad, 8 Ruler, 9 Diverse, 10 Long-leg, 11 Asia, 12 Eft, 14 Mere, 15 Rise, 18 Duo, 21 Oars, 23 Consent, 25 Hamster, 26 Upset, 27 Roomy, 28 Glance.

DOWN: 1 Purple, 2 Silence, 3 Enrolled, 4 Bevy, 5 Ogres, 6 Dee-jay, 7 Adage, 13 Tranquil, 16 Stetson, 17 Mother, 19 Ochre, 20 Statue, 22 Romeo, 24 Stay.

45 —————

ACROSS:1 Abettor, 5 Weigh, 8 Older, 9 Crawler, 10 Affluence, 12 Goa, 13 Quaver, 14 Marble, 17 Apt, 18 Permanent, 20 Termite, 21 Night, 23 Tudor, 24 Tattler.

DOWN: 1 Aroma, 2 End, 3 Torture, 4 Racine, 5 Weave, 6 Illegible, 7 Herbage, 11 Fractured, 13 Quartet, 15 Against, 16 Priest, 18 Prior, 19 Tutor, 22 Gel.

46 —————

ACROSS:1 Know, 3 Nonsense, 9 Khaki, 10 Chinwag, 11 Irk, 13 Privilege, 14 Kitten, 16 Chased, 18 Operation, 20 Yet, 22 Stilton, 23 Prank, 25 Sagacity, 26 Skin.

DOWN: 1 Kukri, 2 Ova, 4 Orchid, 5 Swinish, 6 New jersey, 7 Egghead, 8 Limp, 12 Kettering, 14 Knossos, 15 Elastic, 17 Linnet, 19 Nape, 21 Token, 24 Auk.

47 —————

ACROSS:1 Deacon, 4 Troll, 8 Rated, 9 Residue, 10 Demonic, 11 Brie, 12 End, 14 Stir, 15 Idea, 18 Yen, 21 Avow, 23 Entreat, 25 Proceed, 26 Inane, 27 Nurse, 28 Demean.

DOWN: 1 Dirndl, 2 Attempt, 3 Ordinary, 4 Task, 5 Order, 6 Lieder, 7 Price, 13 Diatribe, 16 Elevate, 17 Dampen, 19 Needy, 20 Strewn, 22 Odour, 24 Mere.

48 —————

ACROSS:1 Shows, 4 Topper, 9 Swindle, 10 Negus, 11 Mink, 12 Nemesis, 13 See, 14 Pail, 16 Nosy, 18 Fat, 20 Prosper, 21 Agra, 24 Abash, 25 Skylark, 26 Shoddy, 27 Hence.

DOWN: 1 Sesame, 2 Orion, 3 Suds, 5 Ointment, 6 Pegasus, 7 Resist, 8 Seine, 13 Slipshod, 15 Avocado, 17 Speaks, 18 Fresh, 19 Tackle, 22 Grain, 23 Myth.

49 —————

ACROSS:1 Pouring, 5 Reign, 8 Renew, 9 Resorts, 10 Excursion, 12 Gag, 13 Polish, 14 Faulty, 17 Emu, 18 Interpret, 20 Scallop, 21 Image, 23 Dress, 24 Dreamed.

DOWN: 1 Purse, 2 Urn, 3 Inwards, 4 Garlic, 5 Rosin, 6 Irregular, 7 Nosegay, 11 Calculate, 13 Pleased, 15 Airline, 16 Stupid, 18 Idles, 19 Trend, 22 Aim.

50 —————

ACROSS:1 Cycle, 4 Logical, 8 Nirvana, 9 Otter, 10 Upset, 11 Holland, 13 Item, 15 Reduce, 17 Impede, 20 Arty, 22 Provoke, 24 Slang, 26 Ocean, 27 Seeping, 28 Dresden, 29 Yield.

DOWN: 1 Conquer, 2 Cares, 3 Elastic, 4 Loathe, 5 Growl, 6 Cottage, 7 Lurid, 12 Omit, 14 Teak, 16 Diocese, 18 Mystery, 19 Engaged, 21 Reason, 22 Proud, 23 Owned, 25 Agile.

51 ————

ACROSS:1 Caught, 4 Rheum, 8 Onion, 9 Adenoid, 10 Proviso, 11 Heal, 12 Nit, 14 Emma, 15 Hoof, 18 Pug, 21 Rice, 23 Acrobat, 25 Condone, 26 Utter, 27 Roomy, 28 Shaded.
DOWN: 1 Choppy, 2 Uniform, 3 Handicap, 4 Reek, 5 Elope, 6 Middle, 7 Bacon, 13 Thorough, 16 Orbited, 17 Bracer, 19 Gavel, 20 Stared, 22 Canto, 24 Pony.

52 ————

ACROSS:1 Therm, 4 Idyll, 10 Hamster, 11 Ample, 12 Curve, 13 Centime, 15 Aged, 17 Abate, 19 Adage, 22 Rome, 25 Dilemma, 27 Leave, 29 Elver, 30 Ingress, 31 Earth, 32 State.
DOWN: 2 Homer, 3 Retreat, 5 Drawn, 6 Lapwing, 7 Shock, 8 Brace, 9 Never, 14 Edam, 16 Germ, 18 Bolivia, 20 Delight, 21 Adder, 23 Oasis, 24 Cease, 26 Merit, 28 Agent.

53 ————

ACROSS:1 Maker, 4 Prophet, 8 Sidecar, 9 Scrub, 10 Caste, 11 Ossicle, 13 Tent, 15 Locust, 17 Orator, 20 Tape, 22 Jocelyn, 24 Slang, 26 Doing, 27 Leitrim, 28 Dresser, 29 Doyen.
DOWN: 1 Musical, 2 Kudos, 3 Rickets, 4 Pardon, 5 Oasis, 6 Haricot, 7 Table, 12 Stop, 14 Etty, 16 Cocaine, 18 Rescind, 19 Regimen, 21 Angler, 22 Jaded, 23 Lagos, 25 Array.

54 ————

ACROSS:7 Deacon, 8 Jested, 10 Certain, 11 Steer, 12 Tool, 13 Sorry, 17 Saint, 18 Silo, 22 Adept, 23 Emerald, 24 Profit, 25 Coping.
DOWN: 1 Educate, 2 Warrior, 3 Nomad, 4 Dessert, 5 Steep, 6 Adorn, 9 Encounter, 14 Captain, 15 Titania, 16 Bondage, 19 Happy, 20 Demon, 21 Felon.

55 ————

ACROSS:1 Bigger, 4 Missed, 7 Greyhound, 9 Helm, 10 Kiwi, 11 Sheep, 13 Podium, 14 Dog-leg, 15 Hiatus, 17 Scampi, 19 Punch, 20 Coop, 22 Ache, 23 Raspberry, 24 Crater, 25 Doodle.
DOWN: 1 Bishop, 2 Germ, 3 Rhythm, 4 Moored, 5 Sink, 6 Daring, 7 Gladiator, 8 Diplomacy, 11 Sun-up, 12 Poach, 15 Hectic, 16 Supper, 17 Screed, 18 Ice age, 21 Pact, 22 Argo.

56 ————

ACROSS:1 Gouda, 4 Gather, 9 Radiant, 10 Stays, 11 Sure, 12 Rotting, 13 Dam, 14 Make, 16 Acre, 18 Pen, 20 Elevate, 21 Pace, 24 Shout, 25 Teacher, 26 Steady, 27 Rusks.
DOWN: 1 Garish, 2 Under, 3 Ajar, 5 Alsatian, 6 Heavier, 7 Resign, 8 Storm, 13 Departed, 15 Awesome, 17 Census, 18 Petty, 19 Debris, 22 Aphis, 23 Fair.

57 ————

ACROSS:1 Centre, 4 Signal, 7 Recovered, 9 Tear, 10 Wash, 11 Perch, 13 Castle, 14 Handel, 15 Incite, 17 Stilts, 19 Exile, 20 Lees, 22 Coma, 23 Deduction, 24 Garble, 25 Depose.
DOWN: 1 Celtic, 2 Tier, 3 Epopee, 4 Stench, 5 Grew, 6 Lethal, 7 Ransacked, 8 Dandelion, 11 Plate, 12 Haste, 15 Idling, 16 Excuse, 17 Slated, 18 Scarce, 21 Serb, 22 Coup.

58 ————

ACROSS:1 Islay, 4 White, 10 Equinox, 11 Unify, 12 Cubit, 13 Redskin, 15 Tray, 17 Igloo, 19 Agate, 22 So-so, 25 Another, 27 Rajah, 29 Fogey, 30 Taloned, 31 Mainz, 32 Waltz.
DOWN: 2 Squib, 3 Annatto, 5 Hound, 6 Thicket, 7 Bench, 8 Extra, 9 Hyena, 14 Eyas, 16 Rose, 18 Georgia, 20 Gorilla, 21 Jaffa, 23 Orate, 24 Shady, 26 Haydn, 28 Janet.

59 ————

ACROSS:1 Author, 4 Docks, 8 Crate, 9 Expense, 10 Donated, 11 Best, 12 Yes, 14 Peak, 15 Idea, 18 Eat, 21 Ever, 23 Egghead, 25 Perhaps, 26 Lithe, 27 Erect, 28 Bridge.
DOWN: 1 Accede, 2 Trainee, 3 Overtake, 4 Dope, 5 Canoe, 6 Siesta, 7 Ready, 13 Singular, 16 Elected, 17 People, 19 Terse, 20 Adhere, 22 Eerie, 24 Last.

60 ————

ACROSS:7 Goethe, 8 Blazes, 10 Imperil, 11 Scene, 12 Tusk, 13 Screw, 17 Rabbi, 18 Neon, 22 Ariel, 23 Leisure, 24 Casual, 25 Reason.
DOWN: 1 Egoists, 2 Tempest, 3 Chart, 4 Cluster, 5 Aztec, 6 Essen, 9 Blackball, 14 Tableau, 15 Bequest, 16 Antenna, 19 Watch, 20 Tipsy, 21 Miser.

61 ————

ACROSS:1 Trays, **4** Shore, **10** Toddler, **11** Aesop, **12** Corgi, **13** Astound, **15** Nest, **17** Soggy, **19** Aside, **22** Ogre, **25** Educate, **27** Count, **29** Erect, **30** Meeting, **31** Stare, **32** Pepys.
DOWN: 2 Rider, **3** Yelling, **5** Heart, **6** Rescued, **7** Stick, **8** Areas, **9** Spade, **14** Star, **16** Eyot, **18** Opulent, **20** Secrete, **21** Jewel, **23** Germs, **24** Stage, **26** Actor, **28** Unity.

62 ————

ACROSS:1 Mocker, **4** Scenes, **7** Slingshot, **9** Alto, **10** Sift, **11** Cider, **13** Sinbad, **14** Modern, **15** Pewter, **17** Fennel, **19** Tiber, **20** Sild, **22** Asia, **23** Laborious, **24** Set off, **25** Elapse.
DOWN: 1 Morass, **2** Kilo, **3** Rancid, **4** System, **5** Eros, **6** Sultan, **7** Stonewall, **8** Tiredness, **11** Cadet, **12** Rover, **15** Pisces, **16** Rip-off, **17** Feline, **18** League, **21** Dado, **22** Aura.

63 ————

ACROSS:1 Piercing, **7** Whale, **8** Co-operate, **9** Dot, **10** Dais, **11** Belfry, **13** Caesar, **14** Craven, **17** Grimly, **18** Brat, **20** Too, **22** Adulation, **23** Relax, **24** Derisory.
DOWN: 1 Paced, **2** Erosive, **3** Chef, **4** Nearer, **5** Bawdy, **6** Pertain, **7** Welfare, **12** Halifax, **13** Cistern, **15** Vertigo, **16** Allure, **17** Godly, **19** Tangy, **21** Sari.

64 ————

ACROSS:1 Derry, **4** Licked, **9** Bravado, **10** Sinew, **11** Iota, **12** Comical, **13** Ash, **14** Drop, **16** I-spy, **18** Lea, **20** Caviare, **21** Scar, **24** Ounce, **25** Serpent, **26** Twenty, **27** Early.
DOWN: 1 Debris, **2** Roast, **3** Year, **5** Insomnia, **6** Kingcup, **7** Dawdle, **8** Coach, **13** Apparent, **15** Revenue, **17** Accost, **18** Least, **19** Pretty, **22** Clear, **23** Brie.

65 ————

ACROSS:1 Table, **4** Wrapper, **8** Problem, **9** Storm, **10** Timer, **11** America, **13** Gate, **15** Ragged, **17** Slayer, **20** Easy, **22** Garment, **24** Refit, **26** Roach, **27** Exclude, **28** Diddled, **29** Light.
DOWN: 1 Tipster, **2** Broom, **3** Enlarge, **4** Wombat, **5** Aisle, **6** Probity, **7** Rumba, **12** Mess, **14** Aden, **16** Garland, **18** Lyrical, **19** Retreat, **21** Attend, **22** Gored, **23** Ethyl, **25** Flung.

66 ————

ACROSS:1 Caldey, **4** Sacks, **8** Sight, **9** Partner, **10** Literal, **11** Gnaw, **12** Lag, **14** Area, **15** Race, **18** Leg, **21** Urge, **23** Lothian, **25** Katydid, **26** Fakir, **27** Rodin, **28** Blithe.
DOWN: 1 Castle, **2** Lighter, **3** External, **4** Surf, **5** Canon, **6** Sprawl, **7** Spill, **13** Grateful, **16** Cricket, **17** Quaker, **19** Glide, **20** Untrue, **22** Gated, **24** Eden.

67 ————

ACROSS:1 Dyers, **4** Traits, **9** Spaniel, **10** Trade, **11** Rate, **12** Palmist, **13** Axe, **14** Open, **16** Stem, **18** Ass, **20** Prudent, **21** Blue, **24** Right, **25** Abridge, **26** Endure, **27** Great.
DOWN: 1 Desire, **2** Exact, **3** Slim, **5** Ruthless, **6** Imagine, **7** Sleuth, **8** Slope, **13** Ancestor, **15** Plugged, **17** Sparse, **18** Atlas, **19** Defect, **22** Ledge, **23** Brag.

68 ————

ACROSS:7 League, **8** Allies, **10** Sundial, **11** Miner, **12** Easy, **13** Abbey, **17** Storm, **18** Past, **22** Bream, **23** Tumbler, **24** Tenant, **25** Groove.
DOWN: 1 Fluster, **2** Varnish, **3** Lurid, **4** Clamber, **5** Fiend, **6** Usurp, **9** Elaborate, **14** Stamina, **15** Walloon, **16** Starter, **19** Abate, **20** Feint, **21** Smirk.

69 ————

ACROSS:1 Sails, **4** Bargain, **8** Chaotic, **9** Poser, **10** Leech, **11** Mediate, **13** Ewer, **15** Rabble, **17** Seance, **20** Ilex, **22** Amphora, **24** Plant, **26** Point, **27** Chemise, **28** Admirer, **29** Spent.
DOWN: 1 Secular, **2** Image, **3** Satchel, **4** Became, **5** Rapid, **6** Abstain, **7** Nerve, **12** Erse, **14** Weir, **16** Baptism, **18** Express, **19** Entreat, **21** Lancer, **22** Alpha, **23** Outer, **25** Agile.

70 ————

ACROSS:7 Planes, **8** Ailing, **10** Trumpet, **11** Midge, **12** Lark, **13** Nanny, **17** Friar, **18** Mere, **22** Gross, **23** Emulate, **24** Rodent, **25** Bistro.
DOWN: 1 Spatula, **2** January, **3** Tempt, **4** Diamond, **5** Giddy, **6** Agree, **9** Stratagem, **14** Present, **15** Penalty, **16** Develop, **19** Aggro, **20** Wordy, **21** Cupid.

71 ————
ACROSS:1 Hanker, 4 Chiefs, 7 Blackmail, 9 Seal, 10 Sure, 11 Level, 13 Method, 14 Learnt, 15 Demise, 17 Cancer, 19 Error, 20 More, 22 Stab, 23 Eradicate, 24 Depend, 25 Renoir.
DOWN: 1 Hansom, 2 Kill, 3 Rocked, 4 Compel, 5 Iris, 6 Silent, 7 Baltimore, 8 Lubricate, 11 Louse, 12 Lehar, 15 Demand, 16 Eroded, 17 Concur, 18 Robber, 21 Erse, 22 Stun.

72 ————
ACROSS:1 Rome, 3 Antiques, 9 Viper, 10 Titanic, 11 Roc, 13 Perimeter, 14 Jalopy, 16 Osiris, 18 Courteous, 20 Lit, 22 Anaemia, 23 Fibre, 25 Sketched, 26 Exit.
DOWN: 1 Rover, 2 Map, 4 Nature, 5 Isthmus, 6 Unnatural, 7 Secures, 8 Grip, 12 Calculate, 14 Jackass, 15 Potomac, 17 Forage, 19 Sofa, 21 Treat, 24 Box.

73 ————
ACROSS:1 Wrecked, 5 Etude, 8 Opera, 9 Launder, 10 Entreat, 11 Agree, 12 Parcel, 14 Depart, 17 Table, 19 Example, 22 Leaning, 23 Acrid, 24 Among, 25 Resolve.
DOWN: 1 Wrote, 2 Elector, 3 Knave, 4 Delete, 5 Educate, 6 Under, 7 Earnest, 12 Patella, 13 Evening, 15 Apparel, 16 Beggar, 18 Beano, 20 Amass, 21 Endue.

74 ————
ACROSS:1 Calmer, 4 Lights, 7 Compliant, 9 Lard, 10 Grip, 11 Greed, 13 Wicket, 14 Runner, 15 Repair, 17 Scipio, 19 Eerie, 20 Bets, 22 Arms, 23 Somnolent, 24 Fluent, 25 Danger.
DOWN: 1 Callow, 2 Mood, 3 Report, 4 Loiter, 5 Gong, 6 Stupor, 7 Crackpots, 8 Transport, 11 Genie, 12 Dunce, 15 Rebuff, 16 Rennet, 17 Sidled, 18 Oyster, 21 Sole, 22 Anon.

75 ————
ACROSS:1 Howe, 3 Peculiar, 9 Broom, 10 Codicil, 11 Yam, 13 Resurgent, 14 Ardour, 16 Novels, 18 Catechism, 20 Tip, 22 Setting, 23 Tutor, 25 Deranged, 26 Deny.
DOWN: 1 Hobby, 2 Woo, 4 Excess, 5 Undergo, 6 Inclement, 7 Relates, 8 Emir, 12 Meditator, 14 Accused, 15 Unction, 17 Single, 19 Mite, 21 Parry, 24 Tie.

76 ————
ACROSS:1 Opinion, 5 Poles, 8 Blend, 9 Advance, 10 Travail, 11 Oasis, 12 Lodger, 14 Maroon, 17 Cider, 19 Traitor, 22 Neglige, 23 Proof, 24 Cater, 25 Sparkle.
DOWN: 1 Orbit, 2 Iceland, 3 India, 4 Nearly, 5 Pavlova, 6 Longs, 7 Stetson, 12 Laconic, 13 Earlier, 15 Outlook, 16 Stress, 18 Digit, 20 Alpha, 21 Rifle.

77 ————
ACROSS:1 Taker, 4 Gander, 9 Trekked, 10 Raped, 11 Hide, 12 Pegasus, 13 Wit, 14 Acer, 16 Tidy, 18 Lie, 20 Intense, 21 Lava, 24 Aural, 25 Plotter, 26 Egress, 27 Macon.
DOWN: 1 Tetchy, 2 Knead, 3 Rake, 5 Arrogate, 6 Deposed, 7 Radish, 8 Adept, 13 Wrinkles, 15 Caterer, 17 Tirade, 18 Leapt, 19 Barren, 22 Antic, 23 Doom.

78 ————
ACROSS:1 Mutton, 4 Bailie, 7 Grotesque, 9 Pyre, 10 Nave, 11 Avail, 13 Coyote, 14 Runner, 15 Feeble, 17 Fiasco, 19 Tumid, 20 Bard, 22 Flay, 23 Directory, 24 Cupola, 25 Remain.
DOWN: 1 Myopic, 2 Tyre, 3 Native, 4 Bestir, 5 Irun, 6 Endear, 7 Greybeard, 8 Earnestly, 11 Atilt, 12 Lurid, 15 Fabric, 16 Eureka, 17 Filter, 18 Oxygen, 21 Dido, 22 From.

79 ————
ACROSS:7 League, 8 Allies, 10 Tonsure, 11 Evade, 12 Over, 13 Beach, 17 Wager, 18 Keen, 22 Alert, 23 Curtail, 24 Strive, 25 Cavern.
DOWN: 1 Elation, 2 Painter, 3 Sun-up, 4 Fluency, 5 Divan, 6 Osier, 9 Reference, 14 Captive, 15 Related, 16 Incline, 19 Raise, 20 Heart, 21 Break.

80 ————
ACROSS:1 Prints, 4 Sepal, 8 Ridge, 9 Holland, 10 Opossum, 11 Tome, 12 Bud, 14 Tsar, 15 Edge, 18 End, 21 Alto, 23 Waiting, 25 Snooker, 26 Agate, 27 Tithe, 28 Defend.
DOWN: 1 Pardon, 2 Indoors, 3 Treasure, 4 Silk, 5 Plato, 6 Ladder, 7 Thumb, 13 Delicate, 16 Grimace, 17 Basset, 19 Dwarf, 20 Agreed, 22 Trout, 24 Skye.

81 ————
ACROSS:1 Allowed, **5** Noise, **8** Lithe, **9** Leeward, **10** Sanctuary, **12** Dew, **13** Parade, **14** Curbed, **17** Pie, **18** Dauntless, **20** Ominous, **21** Uncle, **23** Ennui, **24** Inhaled.
DOWN: 1 Atlas, **2** Lit, **3** Whetted, **4** Dallas, **5** Needy, **6** Inaudible, **7** Endowed, **11** Norwegian, **13** Papoose, **15** Untruth, **16** Muesli, **18** Dhoti, **19** Speed, **22** Col.

82 ————
ACROSS:1 Read, **3** Currents, **9** Vicar, **10** Integer, **11** Lot, **13** Protested, **14** Perish, **16** Strays, **18** Endeavour, **20** Elm, **22** Evening, **23** Comic, **25** Ensemble, **26** Draw.
DOWN: 1 Rival, **2** Arc, **4** Unison, **5** Retreat, **6** Nightmare, **7** Strides, **8** Trip, **12** Tiredness, **14** Precede, **15** Stadium, **17** Mongol, **19** Rich, **21** Macaw, **24** Mar.

83 ————
ACROSS:1 Arbour, **4** Master, **7** Reasoning, **9** Eden, **10** True, **11** Snood, **13** Prompt, **14** Repent, **15** Demure, **17** Pushed, **19** Eclat, **20** Sind, **22** Free, **23** Deception, **24** Tundra, **25** Yelled.
DOWN: 1 Asleep, **2** Omen, **3** Resent, **4** Mentor, **5** Sent, **6** Reject, **7** Recommend, **8** Greenhorn, **11** Spare, **12** Debut, **15** Desist, **16** Eczema, **17** Pantry, **18** Deemed, **21** Dead, **22** Foal.

84 ————
ACROSS:1 Creed, **4** Occur, **10** Ninepin, **11** React, **12** Drown, **13** Ejected, **15** Sure, **17** Often, **19** Rhode, **22** Duke, **25** Pontoon, **27** Sum up, **29** Apart, **30** Idiotic, **31** Decry, **32** Unity.
DOWN: 2 Rondo, **3** Expense, **5** Carve, **6** Unacted, **7** Snide, **8** Anger, **9** Study, **14** Jerk, **16** Undo, **18** Fanfare, **20** Hessian, **21** Sprat, **23** Unfit, **24** Spice, **26** Otter, **28** Motet.

85 ————
ACROSS:1 Centre, **4** Claws, **8** Eaten, **9** Adamant, **10** Shingle, **11** Edge, **12** Rot, **14** Aged, **15** Rome, **18** Era, **21** Sett, **23** Learner, **25** Eyesore, **26** Uncle, **27** Tutor, **28** Desert.
DOWN: 1 Crease, **2** Nothing, **3** Renegade, **4** Crab, **5** Award, **6** Settee, **7** Waver, **13** Treasure, **16** Manacle, **17** Assent, **19** Alien, **20** Ardent, **22** Theft, **24** Poor.

86 ————
ACROSS:1 Sauce, **4** Errors, **9** Refrain, **10** Enter, **11** Watt, **12** Cookery, **13** Oak, **14** Limp, **16** Idle, **18** Arc, **20** Concord, **21** Acme, **24** Ennui, **25** Express, **26** Tasted, **27** Essen.
DOWN: 1 Shrewd, **2** Unfit, **3** Edam, **5** Rhetoric, **6** Oatmeal, **7** Strays, **8** Snack, **13** Opposite, **15** Innings, **17** Accept, **18** Adder, **19** Lesson, **22** Chess, **23** Epee.

87 ————
ACROSS:1 Grate, **4** Scott, **10** Baghdad, **11** Range, **12** Spell, **13** Rhombus, **15** Erne, **17** Metro, **19** Raven, **22** Soon, **25** Crushed, **27** Trait, **29** Opium, **30** Ungodly, **31** Veldt, **32** Faith.
DOWN: 2 Rogue, **3** Tiddler, **5** Cargo, **6** Tenable, **7** Abase, **8** Adorn, **9** Leash, **14** Hero, **16** Rose, **18** Erudite, **20** Antigua, **21** Scoop, **23** Odium, **24** Stays, **26** Humid, **28** Audit.

88 ————
ACROSS:7 Bellow, **8** Stares, **10** Ginseng, **11** Excel, **12** Ibex, **13** Manse, **17** Mirth, **18** Cato, **22** Along, **23** Nemesis, **24** Sermon, **25** Allure.
DOWN: 1 Abigail, **2** Slender, **3** Honey, **4** Atheist, **5** Crack, **6** Psalm, **9** Eglantine, **14** Kingdom, **15** Pass out, **16** Dossier, **19** Passe, **20** Court, **21** Small.

89 ————
ACROSS:1 Grey, **3** Starling, **9** Byron, **10** Resided, **11** Deb, **13** Heartache, **14** Jargon, **16** Jested, **18** Suspicion, **20** Rap, **22** Needier, **23** Vague, **25** Withered, **26** Type.
DOWN: 1 Go bad, **2** Err, **4** Threat, **5** Rosette, **6** Indicator, **7** God-send, **8** Inch, **12** Birds-nest, **14** Just now, **15** Orifice, **17** Fierce, **19** Nova, **21** Piece, **24** Guy.

90 ————
ACROSS:1 Discount, **7** Tents, **8** Woebegone, **9** Rum, **10** Year, **11** Flurry, **13** Jigsaw, **14** Scroll, **17** Swampy, **18** Sten, **20** Lap, **22** Colleague, **23** Sauna, **24** Continue.
DOWN: 1 Dowry, **2** Shebang, **3** Obey, **4** Noodle, **5** Angry, **6** Ishmael, **7** Terrace, **12** Jamaica, **13** Jobless, **15** Octagon, **16** Apollo, **17** Spout, **19** Niece, **21** Vest.

91 ————
ACROSS:1 Odour, 4 Clone, 10 Deposit, 11 Lithe, 12 Extra, 13 Ascribe, 15 Rest, 17 Vista, 19 Omega, 22 Ripe, 25 Missing, 27 Apart, 29 Scent, 30 Orderly, 31 Storm, 32 Tried.
DOWN: 2 Depot, 3 Upstart, 5 Lilac, 6 Nothing, 7 Idler, 8 Atlas, 9 Level, 14 Stop, 16 Earn, 18 Inspect, 20 Meander, 21 Amass, 23 Igloo, 24 Stays, 26 Inter, 28 Aerie.

92 ————
ACROSS:1 Jewel, 4 Purpose, 8 Jezebel, 9 Octet, 10 Tenor, 11 Overrun, 13 Iowa, 15 Unload, 17 Memory, 20 Espy, 22 Acquire, 24 Ethic, 26 Reedy, 27 Inhibit, 28 Warbler, 29 Try-on.
DOWN: 1 Ju-jitsu, 2 Wizen, 3 Liberia, 4 Pillow, 5 Rhone, 6 Ontario, 7 Eaten, 12 Vamp, 14 Oder, 16 Liqueur, 18 Eyeshot, 19 Yucatan, 21 Senior, 22 Arrow, 23 Idyll, 25 Hobby.

93 ————
ACROSS:1 Passed, 4 Tense, 8 Cramp, 9 Rancour, 10 Fatuous, 11 Lees, 12 Try, 14 Kepi, 15 Espy, 18 Awe, 21 Alps, 23 Lampoon, 25 Languid, 26 Nadir, 27 Cache, 28 Hybrid.
DOWN: 1 Pacify, 2 Startle, 3 Euphoria, 4 Tiny, 5 Noose, 6 Egress, 7 Trust, 13 Yeomanry, 16 Prouder, 17 Gallic, 19 Elude, 20 Snared, 22 Punic, 24 Pure.

94 ————
ACROSS:1 Quay, 3 Position, 9 Obese, 10 Devices, 11 Ass, 13 Speedwell, 14 Prompt, 16 Friend, 18 Cathedral, 20 Tot, 22 Amazing, 23 Often, 25 El dorado, 26 Talc.
DOWN: 1 Quota, 2 Ape, 4 Oodles, 5 Invader, 6 Inclement, 7 Nestled, 8 Lees, 12 Shorthand, 14 Pickaxe, 15 Premier, 17 Frigid, 19 Loom, 21 Tonic, 24 Tea.

95 ————
ACROSS:1 Overt, 4 Earned, 9 Trivial, 10 Barge, 11 Arty, 12 Prosaic, 13 Pie, 14 Stir, 16 Item, 18 Tea, 20 Teacher, 21 Skye, 24 Crumb, 25 Parsnip, 26 Sleuth, 27 Boyar.
DOWN: 1 Outlaw, 2 Edict, 3 Toil, 5 Ambrosia, 6 Narrate, 7 Drench, 8 Slope, 13 Prohibit, 15 Traduce, 17 Stocks, 18 Tripe, 19 Keeper, 22 Kinky, 23 Grab.

96 ————
ACROSS:1 Standard, 7 Icing, 8 Passenger, 9 Owl, 10 Dark, 11 Violin, 13 Quango, 14 Snappy, 17 Suture, 18 Clef, 20 Cut, 22 Saltpetre, 23 Locum, 24 Explicit.
DOWN: 1 Sapid, 2 Austria, 3 Deep, 4 Regain, 5 Bison, 6 Agility, 7 Ireland, 12 Egotism, 13 Quickly, 15 Politic, 16 Prolix, 17 Stack, 19 Fleet, 21 Opal.

97 ————
ACROSS:1 Chime, 4 Berlin, 9 Chemist, 10 Gusto, 11 Rill, 12 Cologne, 13 Ask, 14 Area, 16 Need, 18 Act, 20 Impeded, 21 Note, 24 Gouda, 25 Protest, 26 Speaks, 27 Tenor.
DOWN: 1 Cicero, 2 Ideal, 3 Exit, 5 Eggplant, 6 Lasagne, 7 Nooses, 8 Stick, 13 Aardvark, 15 Rapture, 17 Singes, 18 Adept, 19 Better, 22 Ocean, 23 Boot.

98 ————
ACROSS:1 Pastor, 4 Weigh, 8 Turin, 9 Colossi, 10 Optimum, 11 Weed, 12 Pup, 14 Amen, 15 Rude, 18 Tap, 21 Hobo, 23 Adjunct, 25 Risible, 26 Dazed, 27 Haste, 28 Lean-to.
DOWN: 1 Python, 2 Stratum, 3 Ornament, 4 Will, 5 Issue, 6 Hair-do, 7 Scamp, 13 Prejudge, 16 Denizen, 17 Church, 19 Paten, 20 Studio, 22 Basis, 24 Abbe.

99 ————
ACROSS:5 Frank, 8 Einstein, 9 Agape, 10 Scaffold, 11 Sofia, 14 Opt, 16 Elated, 17 Orally, 18 Dip, 20 Abbot, 24 Spurious, 25 Licit, 26 Cicerone, 27 Snags.
DOWN: 1 Tease, 2 Sneak, 3 Stiff, 4 Fillip, 6 Regional, 7 Nuptials, 12 Plebeian, 13 Stooping, 14 Odd, 15 Top, 19 Impair, 21 Gruel, 22 Colon, 23 Askew.

100 ————
ACROSS:7 Cygnet, 8 Chewer, 10 Unhappy, 11 Theme, 12 Liar, 13 Idiom, 17 Peace, 18 Peri, 22 Tithe, 23 Textile, 24 France, 25 Scream.
DOWN: 1 Scruple, 2 Egghead, 3 Tempt, 4 Whatnot, 5 Sweet, 6 Cried, 9 Syndicate, 14 Rebecca, 15 Decibel, 16 Dilemma, 19 Staff, 20 Stray, 21 Exact.

101 ————
ACROSS:1 French, 4 Polish, 7 Merriment, 9 Lied, 10 Grin, 11 Piper, 13 Proust, 14 Dermis, 15 Chilly, 17 Bellow, 19 Metal, 20 Tout, 22 Aura, 23 Shameless, 24 Rotten, 25 Thymus.
DOWN: 1 Fillip, 2 Need, 3 Hermit, 4 Pumped, 5 Lung, 6 Haunts, 7 Melodious, 8 Tremulous, 11 Psalm, 12 Rebel, 15 Cutter, 16 Yeoman, 17 Ballot, 18 Whales, 21 That, 22 Ashy.

102
ACROSS:1 Pecan, 4 Chews, 10 Couplet, 11 Brick, 12 Papaw, 13 Rat-a-tat, 15 Erne, 17 Slide, 19 Offer, 22 None, 25 Lampoon, 27 Rabbi, 29 Stint, 30 Exigent, 31 Agape, 32 Newer.
DOWN: 2 Equip, 3 Allowed, 5 Habit, 6 Whistle, 7 Scape, 8 Stern, 9 Skate, 14 Aeon, 16 Reno, 18 Lemming, 20 Fertile, 21 Clasp, 23 Onset, 24 Ditto, 26 On top, 28 Breve.

103 ————
ACROSS:1 Regions, 5 Treat, 8 Might, 9 Dresden, 10 Assembled, 12 Air, 13 Cogent, 14 Reform, 17 Etc, 18 Billiards, 20 Idolise, 21 Usual, 23 Taste, 24 Scenery.
DOWN: 1 Rumba, 2 Gag, 3 Ottoman, 4 Saddle, 5 Tread, 6 Endeavour, 7 Tantrum, 11 Sagacious, 13 Chemist, 15 Epicure, 16 Aliens, 18 Brine, 19 Silly, 22 Use.

104 ————
ACROSS:1 Holly, 4 Decamps, 8 Liaison, 9 April, 10 Besom, 11 Eastern, 13 Airs, 15 Trunks, 17 Isolde, 20 Loan, 22 Meissen, 24 Optic, 26 Sloop, 27 Awkward, 28 Command, 29 Ruler.
DOWN: 1 Halibut, 2 Loads, 3 Yashmak, 4 Danger, 5 Chaos, 6 Marvell, 7 Salon, 12 Asia, 14 Isle, 16 Uniform, 18 Snooker, 19 Encoder, 21 Onward, 22 Music, 23 Sepia, 25 Trail.

105 ————
ACROSS:1 Bernard, 5 Shore, 8 Needs, 9 Aquifer, 10 Laudatory, 12 Nag, 13 Flaunt, 14 Copied, 17 Boa, 18 Dauntless, 20 Ashamed, 21 Opera, 23 Sidon, 24 Amended.
DOWN: 1 Banal, 2 Rue, 3 Abstain, 4 Deacon, 5 Saucy, 6 Offensive, 7 Enraged, 11 Unabashed, 13 Fabians, 15 Outcome, 16 Buddha, 18 Demon, 19 Shard, 22 End.

106 ————
ACROSS:1 Sheikh, 4 Spear, 8 Preen, 9 Tax-free, 10 Isolate, 11 Brie, 12 Dim, 14 Veto, 15 Adam, 18 Odd, 21 Ally, 23 Rejoice, 25 Midweek, 26 Noble, 27 Reels, 28 Agreed.
DOWN: 1 Sophia, 2 Eyesore, 3 Kangaroo, 4 Saxe, 5 Error, 6 Reefer, 7 Steed, 13 Mah-jongg, 16 Amiable, 17 Farmer, 19 Drake, 20 Depend, 22 Ledge, 24 Bets.

107 ————
ACROSS:7 Severn, 8 Eights, 10 Heroine, 11 Rouge, 12 Loot, 13 Crate, 17 Drift, 18 Itch, 22 Chase, 23 Earnest, 24 Really, 25 Pascal.
DOWN: 1 Asphalt, 2 Everton, 3 Trait, 4 Migrate, 5 Shout, 6 Aster, 9 Terrified, 14 Orderly, 15 Stretch, 16 Shuttle, 19 Acorn, 20 Banal, 21 Organ.

108 ————
ACROSS:1 Rheumy, 4 Nation, 7 Star-gazer, 9 Hypo, 10 Melt, 11 Tenet, 13 Rotter, 14 Double, 15 Twitch, 17 Direct, 19 Hit on, 20 Ache, 22 Asia, 23 Tight-knit, 24 Appear, 25 Really.
DOWN: 1 Rather, 2 Up to, 3 Yorker, 4 Neared, 5 Teem, 6 Nettle, 7 Spotlight, 8 Redbreast, 11 Teach, 12 Toxin, 15 Trauma, 16 Hither, 17 Docker, 18 Trashy, 21 Eire, 22 Aida.

109 ————
ACROSS:1 Litter, 4 Eight, 8 Tears, 9 Elegant, 10 Educate, 11 Idle, 12 Rye, 14 Yeti, 15 Need, 18 Can, 21 Yarn, 23 Overdue, 25 Tedious, 26 Beret, 27 Rinse, 28 Severe.
DOWN: 1 Letter, 2 Traduce, 3 Ecstatic, 4 Ewes, 5 Grand, 6 Tether, 7 Never, 13 Ensemble, 16 Endorse, 17 Oyster, 19 Noise, 20 Beetle, 22 Rodin, 24 Cope.

110 ————
ACROSS:1 Undug, 4 Harwich, 8 Bizarre, 9 Patna, 10 Annul, 11 Assault, 13 Lawn, 15 Denial, 17 Absent, 20 Mope, 22 Outpost, 24 Shred, 26 Okapi, 27 Abdomen, 28 Dilemma, 29 Songs.
DOWN: 1 Upbraid, 2 Dozen, 3 Gorilla, 4 Hee-haw, 5 Ropes, 6 Intrude, 7 Heart, 12 Snap, 14 Alms, 16 Netball, 18 Besides, 19 Tidings, 21 Ottawa, 22 Ovoid, 23 Opium, 25 Roman.

111 ——————
ACROSS:1 Regents, **5** Treat, **8** Frill, **9** Caracas, **10** Expense, **11** Villa, **12** Siesta, **14** Idiocy, **17** Urban, **19** Transom, **22** Terrace, **23** Gaudy, **24** Rated, **25** Masseur.
DOWN: 1 Rifle, **2** Glimpse, **3** Nylon, **4** Sachet, **5** Thrived, **6** Excel, **7** Tuscany, **12** Saunter, **13** Tankard, **15** Obscure, **16** Stream, **18** Beret, **20** Angus, **21** Mayor.

112 ——————
ACROSS:1 Canter, **4** Beret, **8** Cut up, **9** Patella, **10** Read-out, **11** Aria, **12** Eve, **14** Glee, **15** Urdu, **18** Dab, **21** Inch, **23** Athlete, **25** Profess, **26** Realm, **27** Tardy, **28** Bandit.
DOWN: 1 Cicero, **2** Netball, **3** Employed, **4** Bath, **5** Ruler, **6** Tea-bag, **7** Spate, **13** Euphoria, **16** Die-hard, **17** Limpet, **19** Balsa, **20** Helmet, **22** Choir, **24** Levy.

113 ——————
ACROSS:5 Gnash, **8** Terraces, **9** Wrath, **10** Reworded, **11** Japan, **14** Ate, **16** Fallow, **17** Rioter, **18** Lag, **20** Jemmy, **24** Irrigate, **25** Bonny, **26** Insulate, **27** Ascot.
DOWN: 1 Stern, **2** Growl, **3** Carry, **4** Reject, **6** Narrator, **7** Satiated, **12** Ravenous, **13** Flamingo, **14** Awl, **15** Erg, **19** Arrant, **21** Pique, **22** Pagan, **23** Defer.

114 ——————
ACROSS:1 Horrors, **5** Scope, **8** Rebut, **9** Release, **10** Methodist, **12** Get, **13** Beaten, **14** Afraid, **17** Net, **18** Somnolent, **20** Arrival, **21** Shrub, **23** Heady, **24** Memento.
DOWN: 1 Harem, **2** Rib, **3** Outcome, **4** Sordid, **5** Split, **6** Orangeade, **7** Elected, **11** Trattoria, **13** Beneath, **15** Flotsam, **16** Emblem, **18** Savoy, **19** Taboo, **22** Run.

115 ——————
ACROSS:1 Heads, **4** Entails, **8** Retired, **9** Alter, **10** First, **11** Renegue, **13** Crew, **15** Loathe, **17** Emerge, **20** Acre, **22** Capable, **24** Leave, **26** Atoll, **27** Tension, **28** Elevate, **29** Easel.
DOWN: 1 Harmful, **2** Actor, **3** Scratch, **4** Endure, **5** Train, **6** Integer, **7** Serve, **12** Ewer, **14** Real, **16** Approve, **18** Melange, **19** Eternal, **21** Centre, **22** Cease, **23** Balsa, **25** Aries.

116 ——————
ACROSS:1 Polished, **7** Irene, **8** Lethargic, **9** Yam, **10** Sour, **11** Anubis, **13** Cheery, **14** Trying, **17** Covert, **18** Wing, **20** Rue, **22** Talkative, **23** Ovate, **24** Examples.
DOWN: 1 Pelts, **2** Lettuce, **3** Sham, **4** Engine, **5** Pepys, **6** Lemming, **7** Iceberg, **12** Private, **13** Cheroot, **15** Initial, **16** Prolix, **17** Cedar, **19** Guess, **21** Calm.

117 ——————
ACROSS:7 Tennis, **8** Racket, **10** Relieve, **11** Delhi, **12** Last, **13** Ditty, **17** Civil, **18** Epic, **22** Swell, **23** Upsilon, **24** Impose, **25** Magnum.
DOWN: 1 Sterile, **2** Analyse, **3** Hives, **4** Mandate, **5** Skull, **6** Stoic, **9** Seditious, **14** Aimless, **15** Opulent, **16** Economy, **19** Aspic, **20** Tempt, **21** Oscar.

118 ——————
ACROSS:1 Stand-in, **5** Rheum, **8** Reset, **9** Tessera, **10** Panther, **11** Royal, **12** Decide, **14** Versus, **17** Visor, **19** Habitat, **22** Omnibus, **23** Waned, **24** Sedge, **25** Lyrical.
DOWN: 1 Strap, **2** Arsenic, **3** Ditch, **4** Nature, **5** Reserve, **6** Elegy, **7** Measles, **12** Devious, **13** Durable, **15** Satanic, **16** Chisel, **18** Synod, **20** Bower, **21** Tidal.

119 ——————
ACROSS:1 Marry, **4** Thyme, **10** Matisse, **11** Annex, **12** Serve, **13** Restive, **15** Crop, **17** Write, **19** Icing, **22** Arch, **25** Console, **27** Allot, **29** Prove, **30** Legatee, **31** Brink, **32** Adorn.
DOWN: 2 Actor, **3** Respect, **5** Heaps, **6** Mansion, **7** Amuse, **8** Metro, **9** Excel, **14** Epic, **16** Real, **18** Rancour, **20** Changed, **21** Scope, **23** Reply, **24** Steep, **26** Ocean, **28** Later.

120 ——————
ACROSS:5 Ghyll, **8** Tea-party, **9** Droll, **10** Mosquito, **11** Limit, **14** Wet, **16** Sailor, **17** Orator, **18** Yap, **20** Crypt, **24** Pheasant, **25** Idaho, **26** Envisage, **27** Trade.
DOWN: 1 Stump, **2** Lasso, **3** Value, **4** Statue, **6** Harridan, **7** Lollipop, **12** Labrador, **13** Slipshod, **14** Wry, **15** Top, **19** Athens, **21** Rapid, **22** Canal, **23** Steer.

121 ————
ACROSS:1 Column, **4** Behan, **8** Legal, **9** Trailer, **10** Cuticle, **11** Etna, **12** Web, **14** Oral, **15** Rape, **18** Erg, **21** Hope, **23** Receive, **25** Auction, **26** Brave, **27** Hedge, **28** Streak.
DOWN: 1 Calico, **2** Lighter, **3** Molecule, **4** Beak, **5** Helot, **6** Normal, **7** Strew, **13** Brickbat, **16** Primate, **17** Thrash, **19** Grant, **20** Bedeck, **22** Paced, **24** Jive.

122 ————
ACROSS:1 Probe, **4** Bubble, **9** Artless, **10** Beast, **11** Corn, **12** Emotion, **13** Fur, **14** Trio, **16** Edge, **18** Inn, **20** Eastern, **21** Pair, **24** Igloo, **25** Nothing, **26** Treaty, **27** Right.
DOWN: 1 Plaice, **2** Otter, **3** Ever, **5** Unbroken, **6** Bearing, **7** Extend, **8** Osier, **13** Foremost, **15** Resolve, **17** Resist, **18** Inane, **19** Fright, **22** Aping, **23** Stir.

123 ————
ACROSS:1 Aside, **4** Oppress, **8** Trigger, **9** Quake, **10** Sinai, **11** Sweater, **13** Sash, **15** Nought, **17** Acacia, **20** Oath, **22** Disarms, **24** Equip, **26** Roast, **27** Another, **28** Citadel, **29** Tyrol.
DOWN: 1 Artisan, **2** Ixion, **3** English, **4** Ogress, **5** Pique, **6** Elastic, **7** Spear, **12** What, **14** Atom, **16** Upstart, **18** Cheroot, **19** Apparel, **21** Assail, **22** Doric, **23** Rated, **25** Usher.

124 ————
ACROSS:7 Potato, **8** Flower, **10** Reprove, **11** Cargo, **12** Deny, **13** Cured, **17** Sloth, **18** Aden, **22** Admit, **23** Requiem, **24** Carnal, **25** Basalt.
DOWN: 1 Upgrade, **2** Stipend, **3** Stoop, **4** Slacken, **5** Swore, **6** Proof, **9** Desultory, **14** Flotsam, **15** Admiral, **16** Animate, **19** Sauce, **20** Smirk, **21** Squaw.

125 ————
ACROSS:7 Latter, **8** Chewed, **10** Strange, **11** Rinse, **12** Open, **13** Lemon, **17** Storm, **18** Wren, **22** Obese, **23** Trivial, **24** Bleach, **25** Brahms.
DOWN: 1 Blossom, **2** Started, **3** Jeans, **4** Pharaoh, **5** Swing, **6** Adder, **9** Penetrate, **14** Stretch, **15** Freight, **16** Endless, **19** Doubt, **20** Jewel, **21** Fiord.

126 ————
ACROSS:1 Barber, **4** Queue, **8** Lucre, **9** Ruinous, **10** Erupted, **11** Byre, **12** Elk, **14** Jeer, **15** Alps, **18** Spa, **21** Loco, **23** Laggard, **25** Creeper, **26** Rouse, **27** Delft, **28** Posset.
DOWN: 1 Bullet, **2** Recluse, **3** Electors, **4** Quit, **5** Ebony, **6** Ensued, **7** Pride, **13** Kangaroo, **16** Plagues, **17** Placed, **19** Alarm, **20** Advert, **22** Creel, **24** Spit.

127 ————
ACROSS:1 Beaux, **4** Belles, **9** Farrago, **10** Toxic, **11** Lush, **12** Treacle, **13** Moo, **14** Up to, **16** Cony, **18** Ash, **20** Bezique, **21** Tact, **24** Salmi, **25** Irksome, **26** Didcot, **27** Theft.
DOWN: 1 Befall, **2** Arras, **3** Xray, **5** Entrench, **6** Lexicon, **7** Sicken, **8** Motto, **13** Mosquito, **15** Puzzled, **17** Abused, **18** Aegis, **19** Attest, **22** Adobe, **23** Skit.

128 ————
ACROSS:1 Satyr, **4** Light, **10** Beneath, **11** Erase, **12** Doyen, **13** Untried, **15** Edge, **17** Trade, **19** Every, **22** Fade, **25** Artists, **27** Rogue, **29** Clean, **30** Edifice, **31** Steep, **32** Atoll.
DOWN: 2 Annoy, **3** Yearned, **5** Inert, **6** Heavier, **7** Abode, **8** Shrug, **9** Ready, **14** Need, **16** Deft, **18** Retreat, **20** Verdict, **21** Lance, **23** Ashen, **24** Beret, **26** Sense, **28** Grill.

129 ————
ACROSS:1 Chase, **4** Tonnes, **9** Spanner, **10** Three, **11** Eyed, **12** Compare, **13** Foe, **14** Ogre, **16** Sped, **18** Cot, **20** Scourge, **21** Solo, **24** Rinse, **25** Student, **26** Repose, **27** Tenor.
DOWN: 1 Cashew, **2** Amaze, **3** Erne, **5** Optimist, **6** Narrate, **7** Sweden, **8** Price, **13** Fearless, **15** Grown-up, **17** Usurer, **18** Cease, **19** Doctor, **22** Ocean, **23** Just.

130 ————
ACROSS:1 Chile, **4** Weather, **8** Aviator, **9** Inset, **10** Tudor, **11** Laggard, **13** Apex, **15** Rabble, **17** Impede, **20** Also, **22** Greatly, **24** Copse, **26** Upset, **27** Inertia, **28** Address, **29** Yeast.
DOWN: 1 Charter, **2** Iliad, **3** Enthral, **4** Warble, **5** Aping, **6** Hostage, **7** Rated, **12** Axis, **14** Peal, **16** Blessed, **18** Mockery, **19** Elegant, **21** Lyrics, **22** Gouda, **23** Title, **25** Patna.

131 —————
ACROSS: 1 Mosque, 4 Quito, 8 Laird, 9 Spinoza, 10 Esparto, 11 Esau, 12 New, 14 Trio, 15 Iota, 18 Gnu, 21 Easy, 23 Reduced, 25 Perfume, 26 Irate, 27 Extol, 28 Debate.
DOWN: 1 Mildew, 2 Slipper, 3 Underdog, 4 Quit, 5 Irons, 6 Opaque, 7 Aston, 13 Windpipe, 16 Toccata, 17 People, 19 Urged, 20 Adhere, 22 Sprat, 24 Gull.

132 —————
ACROSS: 1 Belle, 4 Weather, 8 Spartan, 9 Saved, 10 Lathe, 11 Emperor, 13 Acre, 15 Dearth, 17 Spider, 20 Ouse, 22 Redrawn, 24 Await, 26 Large, 27 Trapper, 28 Denoted, 29 Tweed.
DOWN: 1 Bustled, 2 Least, 3 Entreat, 4 Winner, 5 Aesop, 6 Hovered, 7 Rider, 12 Mess, 14 Chow, 16 Andiron, 18 Peasant, 19 Retired, 21 United, 22 Ruled, 23 Avert, 25 Ample.

133 —————
ACROSS: 1 Crewel, 4 Streak, 7 Hopscotch, 9 Deed, 10 Hang, 11 Slick, 13 Rarity, 14 Hearty, 15 Rufous, 17 Action, 19 Myrrh, 20 Pelt, 22 Acer, 23 Transpire, 24 Timely, 25 Tallow.
DOWN: 1 Condor, 2 Wood, 3 Lastly, 4 Scorch, 5 Rich, 6 Kingly, 7 Heartfelt, 8 Hair-piece, 11 Strum, 12 Ketch, 15 Report, 16 Sydney, 17 Armpit, 18 Narrow, 21 True, 22 Aral.

134 —————
ACROSS: 7 Misses, 8 Beaten, 10 Elation, 11 Title, 12 Seen, 13 Worry, 17 Extra, 18 Dear, 22 Bloom, 23 Chemist, 24 Usable, 25 Docile.
DOWN: 1 Immense, 2 Escaped, 3 Begin, 4 Western, 5 State, 6 Under, 9 Incorrect, 14 Example, 15 Deficit, 16 Trotter, 19 About, 20 Nomad, 21 Felon.

135 —————
ACROSS: 1 Crank, 4 Handel, 9 Reading, 10 Clang, 11 Oust, 12 Purport, 13 Toe, 14 Isle, 16 Tint, 18 Fee, 20 Stipple, 21 Camp, 24 Eager, 25 Statute, 26 Tirade, 27 Breve.
DOWN: 1 Carton, 2 Amass, 3 Knit, 5 Accurate, 6 Dragoon, 7 Legate, 8 Agape, 13 Tempered, 15 Snigger, 17 Aspect, 18 Feast, 19 Sphere, 22 Amuse, 23 Lamb.

136 —————
ACROSS: 1 Read, 3 Herrings, 9 Colic, 10 Unmoved, 11 Rib, 13 Monologue, 14 Animal, 16 Gratis, 18 Pesticide, 20 Rag, 22 Ironing, 23 Idiom, 25 Teetered, 26 Skin.
DOWN: 1 Recur, 2 Awl, 4 Equine, 5 Rambler, 6 Navigator, 7 Sadness, 8 Scum, 12 Brimstone, 14 Appoint, 15 Asinine, 17 Single, 19 Epic, 21 Gamin, 24 Irk.

137 —————
ACROSS: 7 Asthma, 8 Tickle, 10 Bonanza, 11 Tulip, 12 Grin, 13 Scorn, 17 Verse, 18 Here, 22 Leech, 23 Exclude, 24 Biceps, 25 Corset.
DOWN: 1 Cabbage, 2 Stand-in, 3 Amend, 4 Disturb, 5 Skill, 6 Tempt, 9 Lancaster, 14 Perhaps, 15 Request, 16 Memento, 19 Globe, 20 Teach, 21 Actor.

138 —————
ACROSS: 5 Would, 8 Hyacinth, 9 Beano, 10 Ricochet, 11 Scald, 14 Sty, 16 Carafe, 17 Assent, 18 Tom, 20 Fatal, 24 Stiletto, 25 Moron, 26 Singular, 27 Maybe.
DOWN: 1 Shire, 2 Watch, 3 Hitch, 4 Street, 6 Overcast, 7 Lanoline, 12 Paranoia, 13 Catacomb, 14 Set, 15 Yam, 19 Outfit, 21 Elegy, 22 Stole, 23 Board.

139 —————
ACROSS: 1 Ruff, 3 Draughts, 9 Gower, 10 Burglar, 11 Yew, 13 Glengarry, 14 Detach, 16 Stroud, 18 Marinated, 20 Sew, 22 Globule, 23 Wince, 25 Doorstep, 26 Swat.
DOWN: 1 Rugby, 2 Few, 4 Rabies, 5 Upright, 6 Hilarious, 7 Strayed, 8 Trug, 12 Water-polo, 14 Damaged, 15 Concuss, 17 Athene, 19 Down, 21 Wheat, 24 New.

140 —————
ACROSS: 1 German, 4 Eight, 8 Ample, 9 Laconic, 10 Inexact, 11 Well, 12 Hot, 14 Real, 15 Eddy, 18 Eat, 21 Rush, 23 Almoner, 25 Chaucer, 26 Noise, 27 Rifle, 28 Assent.
DOWN: 1 Gratis, 2 Replete, 3 Amenable, 4 Each, 5 Genre, 6 Tickle, 7 Cloth, 13 Terminus, 16 Dentine, 17 Grocer, 19 Tarry, 20 Ardent, 22 Staff, 24 Acre.

141 ———
ACROSS:1 Forth, **4** Estate, **9** Charter, **10** Caned, **11** Damp, **12** Crimson, **13** Lie, **14** Ache, **16** Toad, **18** Buy, **20** Clipper, **21** Char, **24** Tower, **25** Keratin, **26** Engage, **27** Pulse.
DOWN: 1 Facade, **2** Realm, **3** Hate, **5** Sacristy, **6** Amnesia, **7** Ending, **8** Grace, **13** Leapfrog, **15** Chinwag, **17** Scythe, **18** Brake, **19** Prince, **22** Hotel, **23** Prop.

142 ———
ACROSS:1 Strait, **4** Fights, **7** Precedent, **9** Sway, **10** Grab, **11** Elver, **13** Desire, **14** Ravage, **15** Lunacy, **17** Dither, **19** Tepid, **20** Cage, **22** Arid, **23** Emergency, **24** Energy, **25** Twelve.
DOWN: 1 Soused, **2** Airy, **3** Tackle, **4** Fodder, **5** Gang, **6** Stable, **7** Parsonage, **8** Treachery, **11** Erect, **12** Rabid, **15** Locate, **16** Yearly, **17** Digest, **18** Riddle, **21** Emir, **22** Acne.

143 ———
ACROSS:1 Peek, **3** District, **9** Rough, **10** Plaster, **11** Add, **13** Erroneous, **14** Pirate, **16** Groups, **18** Eiderdown, **20** Eye, **22** Envelop, **23** Crewe, **25** Talisman, **26** Best.
DOWN: 1 Parka, **2** Emu, **4** Import, **5** Trainer, **6** Introduce, **7** Thrusts, **8** Shoe, **12** Daredevil, **14** Prefect, **15** Turtles, **17** Hoopla, **19** Nick, **21** Event, **24** Ewe.

144 ———
ACROSS:1 Alights, **5** Upper, **8** Synod, **9** Ruinous, **10** Pattern, **11** Infer, **12** Codify, **14** Vellum, **17** Pagan, **19** Auditor, **22** Travail, **23** Equal, **24** Lisle, **25** Tellers.
DOWN: 1 Aesop, **2** Ignited, **3** Hedge, **4** String, **5** Utilise, **6** Proof, **7** Rostrum, **12** Capital, **13** Fanfare, **15** Lettuce, **16** Wallet, **18** Grass, **20** Dwell, **21** Rolls.

145 ———
ACROSS:1 Knight, **4** Traits, **7** Sweet shop, **9** Pawn, **10** Grub, **11** Joker, **13** Rafter, **14** Lancet, **15** Winnow, **17** Bandit, **19** Nicer, **20** Toss, **22** Prow, **23** Spectacle, **24** Elated, **25** Lately.
DOWN: 1 Kipper, **2** Gown, **3** Tremor, **4** Tassel, **5** Agog, **6** Sorbet, **7** Swiftness, **8** Procedure, **11** Jeton, **12** Radar, **15** Wattle, **16** Winced, **17** Bewail, **18** Tawdry, **21** Spot, **22** Plot.

146 ———
ACROSS:1 Inveigh, **5** Sedge, **8** Pixie, **9** Magical, **10** Limitless, **12** Map, **13** Cellar, **14** Remote, **17** Bad, **18** Apprehend, **20** Rooster, **21** Error, **23** Tutor, **24** Satiety.
DOWN: 1 Impel, **2** Vex, **3** Inertia, **4** Hamlet, **5** Sages, **6** Decompose, **7** Eclipse, **11** Maladroit, **13** Cabaret, **15** Everest, **16** Sports, **18** Alter, **19** Dirty, **22** Rue.

147 ———
ACROSS:5 Allay, **8** Dismayed, **9** Snare, **10** Practice, **11** Aside, **14** Art, **16** Roller, **17** Ormolu, **18** Cry, **20** Eject, **24** Ambience, **25** Truro, **26** Autobahn, **27** Tramp.
DOWN: 1 Adept, **2** Essay, **3** Cacti, **4** Fencer, **6** Lonesome, **7** Airedale, **12** Conjurer, **13** Plectrum, **14** Arc, **15** Toy, **19** Rumour, **21** Minor, **22** Sneak, **23** Penny.

148 ———
ACROSS:1 Santa, **4** Claws, **10** Asperse, **11** Ideal, **12** Salve, **13** Sighted, **15** Need, **17** Coats, **19** Often, **22** Able, **25** Amateur, **27** After, **29** China, **30** Saffron, **31** Enrol, **32** Algol.
DOWN: 2 Appal, **3** Torrent, **5** Lying, **6** Wrestle, **7** Cause, **8** Dense, **9** Glade, **14** Idol, **16** Esau, **18** Ovation, **20** Fearful, **21** Sauce, **23** Brash, **24** Prank, **26** Erato, **28** Torso.

149 ———
ACROSS:1 Gains, **4** Borough, **8** Upstart, **9** Dogma, **10** Minor, **11** Earnest, **13** Oast, **15** Thrown, **17** Orator, **20** Name, **22** Thermal, **24** Paris, **26** Adieu, **27** Glimmer, **28** Augment, **29** Alarm.
DOWN: 1 Gourmet, **2** Ibsen, **3** Sparrow, **4** Bathes, **5** Rider, **6** Unguent, **7** Heart, **12** Atom, **14** Anna, **16** Reeling, **18** Replica, **19** Rostrum, **21** Alight, **22** Tiara, **23** Mauve, **25** Rumba.

150 ———
ACROSS:1 Chukker, **5** Routs, **8** Avert, **9** Tableau, **10** Matchless, **12** Ran, **13** Scrape, **14** Lather, **17** Ass, **18** Distended, **20** Provide, **21** Apron, **23** Ridge, **24** Tremble.
DOWN: 1 Claim, **2** Ure, **3** Ketchup, **4** Rather, **5** Rebus, **6** Unearthed, **7** Stunner, **11** Threshold, **13** Scarper, **15** Average, **16** Assert, **18** Drive, **19** Dunce, **22** Rob.

151 ────────
ACROSS:1 Mall, **3** Practise, **9** Jewel, **10** Corunna, **11** Rut, **13** Represent, **14** Juggle, **16** Deeply, **18** Intention, **20** Ram, **22** Implant, **23** Wispy, **25** Gathered, **26** Spur.
DOWN: 1 Major, **2** Law, **4** Recipe, **5** Cortege, **6** Innkeeper, **7** Exactly, **8** Slur, **12** Tight spot, **14** Joining, **15** Lineage, **17** Virtue, **19** News, **21** Mayor, **24** Sap.

152 ────────
ACROSS:1 Pence, **4** Hills, **10** Arrange, **11** Leave, **12** Cargo, **13** Grown-up, **15** Line, **17** Eager, **19** Adorn, **22** Ogre, **25** Neptune, **27** Claim, **29** About, **30** Skipper, **31** Berry, **32** Cello.
DOWN: 2 Error, **3** Console, **5** Igloo, **6** Learner, **7** Catch, **8** Reign, **9** Heaps, **14** Rear, **16** Iron, **18** Approve, **20** Deceive, **21** Knead, **23** Geese, **24** Smart, **26** Utter, **28** Appal.

153 ────────
ACROSS:1 Polished, **7** Irene, **8** Capricorn, **9** Ill, **10** Soil, **11** Agreed, **13** Dagger, **14** Psyche, **17** Allure, **18** Smut, **20** Sum, **22** Catchword, **23** Tosca, **24** Drudgery.
DOWN: 1 Paces, **2** Lapwing, **3** Skin, **4** Enough, **5** Tepid, **6** Recluse, **7** Incense, **12** Replica, **13** Density, **15** Compose, **16** Writer, **17** Amuse, **19** Toddy, **21** Shed.

154 ────────
ACROSS:1 Fought, **4** Worth, **8** Lords, **9** Chaotic, **10** Eminent, **11** Trio, **12** Eli, **14** Beau, **15** Gibe, **18** Sad, **21** Lido, **23** Erosive, **25** Crofter, **26** Idiot, **27** Doing, **28** Cypher.
DOWN: 1 Falter, **2** Ukraine, **3** Hesperus, **4** Weak, **5** Rotor, **6** Hector, **7** Acute, **13** Ignominy, **16** British, **17** Placid, **19** Decry, **20** Fetter, **22** Dhoti, **24** Stag.

155 ────────
ACROSS:7 Asthma, **8** Tickle, **10** Acrylic, **11** Titan, **12** Tier, **13** Canoe, **17** Panic, **18** Prop, **22** Lucid, **23** Officer, **24** Frisky, **25** Bisect.
DOWN: 1 Canasta, **2** Starter, **3** Smell, **4** Fiction, **5** Skate, **6** Seine, **9** Scrap-iron, **14** Vandyke, **15** Proceed, **16** Operate, **19** Bluff, **20** Acrid, **21** Affix.

156 ────────
ACROSS:1 Steak, **4** Acclaim, **8** Gavotte, **9** Speak, **10** Earth, **11** Swelter, **13** Ewer, **15** Tyrone, **17** Abides, **20** Lope, **22** Rickets, **24** Torso, **26** Bliss, **27** Rambler, **28** Trellis, **29** Sedan.
DOWN: 1 Suggest, **2** Elver, **3** Kitchen, **4** Averse, **5** Caste, **6** Abetted, **7** Maker, **12** Wrap, **14** Welt, **16** Receive, **18** Betimes, **19** Sporran, **21** Osiris, **22** Robot, **23** Easel, **25** Riled.

157 ────────
ACROSS:1 Tester, **4** Tricks, **7** Archangel, **9** Lino, **10** Meat, **11** Waver, **13** Trader, **14** Rarely, **15** Jocose, **17** Fiddly, **19** Hated, **20** Vain, **22** Eros, **23** Certainly, **24** Lackey, **25** Heaven.
DOWN: 1 Tablet, **2** Tyro, **3** Rehear, **4** Tanker, **5** Item, **6** Scatty, **7** Antarctic, **8** Legendary, **11** Welsh, **12** Rapid, **15** Jovial, **16** Earthy, **17** Fetish, **18** Yes-men, **21** Neck, **22** Elia.

158 ────────
ACROSS:1 Queue, **4** Weight, **9** Awesome, **10** Under, **11** Note, **12** Siamese, **13** Ape, **14** Arid, **16** Erse, **18** End, **20** Pensive, **21** Late, **24** Aloft, **25** Inspect, **26** Stride, **27** After.
DOWN: 1 Quaint, **2** Erect, **3** Eton, **5** Educated, **6** Goddess, **7** Tureen, **8** Cease, **13** Admitted, **15** Rancour, **17** Spears, **18** Eerie, **19** Better, **22** Agent, **23** Asia.

159 ────────
ACROSS:1 Drummer, **5** Dairy, **8** Leeds, **9** Iceberg, **10** Apprehend, **12** Emu, **13** Deride, **14** Repast, **17** Soh, **18** Sarcastic, **20** Annuity, **21** Lydia, **23** Tenet, **24** Network.
DOWN: 1 Delta, **2** Ure, **3** Misdeed, **4** Raider, **5** Dread, **6** Inelegant, **7** Yoghurt, **11** Parthenon, **13** Distant, **15** Epaulet, **16** Crayon, **18** Swift, **19** Crack, **22** Duo.

160 ────────
ACROSS:5 House, **8** Swarming, **9** Fable, **10** Unctuous, **11** Booty, **14** Sty, **16** Tenure, **17** Aviary, **18** Ask, **20** Coypu, **24** Croupier, **25** Hobby, **26** Backward, **27** Osier.
DOWN: 1 Issue, **2** Fancy, **3** Amour, **4** Unjust, **6** Oratorio, **7** Salutary, **12** Decorous, **13** Culpable, **14** Sea, **15** Yak, **19** Spread, **21** Lucky, **22** Milan, **23** Crude.

161
ACROSS:**1** Whacks, **4** Works, **8** Expel, **9** Engaged, **10** Caraway, **11** Flat, **12** Lid, **14** Gnat, **15** Oval, **18** Tea, **21** Urdu, **23** Concede, **25** Prosper, **26** Amour, **27** Relax, **28** Stress.
DOWN: **1** Wretch, **2** Aspirin, **3** Kilowatt, **4** Wage, **5** Rigel, **6** Sedate, **7** Beryl, **13** Downcast, **16** Anemone, **17** Bumper, **19** Acorn, **20** Debris, **22** Droll, **24** Apex.

162
ACROSS:**7** Cutter, **8** Figure, **10** Upright, **11** Iraqi, **12** Reef, **13** Pique, **17** Scope, **18** Coma, **22** Trait, **23** Apostle, **24** Rusted, **25** Banner.
DOWN: **1** Acquire, **2** Starter, **3** Hedge, **4** Minimum, **5** Mural, **6** Begin, **9** Ethiopian, **14** Scatter, **15** Contend, **16** Madeira, **19** Stern, **20** Waist, **21** Nomad.

163
ACROSS:**1** Mist, **3** Stickily, **9** Tiger, **10** Visible, **11** Red, **13** Threefold, **14** Cup-tie, **16** Angled, **18** Press-gang, **20** Oak, **22** Cascade, **23** Lodge, **25** Toddling, **26** Boil.
DOWN: **1** Meter, **2** Sag, **4** Tavern, **5** Cistern, **6** Imbroglio, **7** Yielded, **8** Grit, **12** Depressed, **14** Copy-cat, **15** Install, **17** Cavern, **19** Gold, **21** Knell, **24** Duo.

164
ACROSS:**5** Toxin, **8** Spectres, **9** Gaunt, **10** Armagnac, **11** Touch, **14** Let, **16** Palace, **17** Orient, **18** Guy, **20** Study, **24** Province, **25** Probe, **26** Wanderer, **27** Later.
DOWN: **1** Essay, **2** Seems, **3** Stage, **4** Decade, **6** Oratorio, **7** Innocent, **12** Bacteria, **13** Laudable, **14** Leg, **15** Toy, **19** Uproar, **21** Evade, **22** Angry, **23** Beard.

165
ACROSS:**1** Fasten, **4** Hating, **7** Catamaran, **9** Gold, **10** Pelt, **11** Elite, **13** Remedy, **14** Savage, **15** Forget, **17** Albino, **19** Sabre, **20** Loud, **22** Hurt, **23** Sometimes, **24** Modest, **25** Expert.
DOWN: **1** Finger, **2** Toad, **3** Nearly, **4** Hearts, **5** Trap, **6** Gentle, **7** Clamorous, **8** Nefarious, **11** Edges, **12** Eagle, **15** Fulham, **16** Talent, **17** Arrive, **18** Outfit, **21** Done, **22** Help.

166
ACROSS:**1** Raining, **5** Queen, **8** Paean, **9** Evasive, **10** Deference, **12** Ill, **13** Greedy, **14** Tabard, **17** Bag, **18** Blameless, **20** Leisure, **21** Inane, **23** Digit, **24** Tersely.
DOWN: **1** Rapid, **2** Ire, **3** Ignored, **4** Greens, **5** Quake, **6** Eliminate, **7** Needled, **11** Fledgling, **13** Gobbled, **15** Atelier, **16** Caveat, **18** Blunt, **19** Seedy, **22** Awe.

167
ACROSS:**1** Whole, **4** Sailors, **8** Lobelia, **9** Green, **10** Alter, **11** Totally, **13** Grab, **15** Yankee, **17** Elapse, **20** Soya, **22** Society, **24** Sugar, **26** Amend, **27** Tugboat, **28** Post-war, **29** Attic.
DOWN: **1** Wallaby, **2** Orbit, **3** Enlarge, **4** Sparta, **5** Ingot, **6** Overlap, **7** Sunny, **12** Obey, **14** Rest, **16** Nucleus, **18** Lasagna, **19** Erratic, **21** Oyster, **22** Scamp, **23** Endow, **25** Ghost.

168
ACROSS:**1** Comfort, **5** Table, **8** Beast, **9** Release, **10** Rebellion, **12** Era, **13** Spring, **14** Breeze, **17** Oaf, **18** Repressed, **20** Pickled, **21** India, **23** Rider, **24** Regimen.
DOWN: **1** Caber, **2** Moa, **3** Ortolan, **4** Torpid, **5** Talon, **6** Blameless, **7** Elevate, **11** Barefaced, **13** Snooper, **15** Reeling, **16** Spider, **18** Ruler, **19** Drawn, **22** Dam.

169
ACROSS:**1** Delicate, **7** Essen, **8** Cataclysm, **9** Rue, **10** Rare, **11** Entrap, **13** Yellow, **14** Studio, **17** Falcon, **18** Over, **20** Hur, **22** Gradually, **23** Runny, **24** Betrayal.
DOWN: **1** Decor, **2** Lateral, **3** Cock, **4** Trying, **5** Usurp, **6** Inferno, **7** Emirate, **12** Zoology, **13** Yoghurt, **15** Devilry, **16** Morale, **17** Frank, **19** Royal, **21** Burr.

170
ACROSS:**1** Choker, **4** Light, **8** Niece, **9** Amateur, **10** Adamant, **11** Stun, **12** Hit, **14** Blue, **15** Ally, **18** Din, **21** Edam, **23** Epistle, **25** Adhered, **26** Usual, **27** Tense, **28** Intend.
DOWN: **1** Cancan, **2** Overall, **3** Elevated, **4** Load, **5** Guest, **6** Throng, **7** Faith, **13** Taciturn, **16** Lettuce, **17** Depart, **19** Needy, **20** Healed, **22** Ashen, **24** Free.

171
ACROSS: 1 Deacon, 4 Trolls, 7 Embarrass, 9 Dune, 10 Tang, 11 Scrap, 13 Noodle, 14 Career, 15 Summer, 17 Canute, 19 Koran, 20 Lens, 22 Free, 23 Threshold, 24 Tippet, 25 Wintry.
DOWN: 1 Deaden, 2 Come, 3 Nuance, 4 Tarmac, 5 Oast, 6 Singer, 7 Enjoyment, 8 Safeguard, 11 Sleek, 12 Pagan, 15 Silent, 16 Rodent, 17 Cashew, 18 Energy, 21 Ship, 22 Flan.

172
ACROSS: 1 Sealing, 5 Tiles, 8 Iraqi, 9 Auditor, 10 Decimal, 11 Egret, 12 Geyser, 14 Stench, 17 Adapt, 19 Apostle, 22 Obscure, 23 Fauna, 24 Range, 25 Torment.
DOWN: 1 Spied, 2 Anarchy, 3 Ilium, 4 Gladly, 5 Tidiest, 6 Later, 7 Scratch, 12 Glamour, 13 Enthuse, 15 Netsuke, 16 Latent, 18 Arson, 20 Offer, 21 Exact.

173
ACROSS: 1 Hart, 3 Breakers, 9 Ledge, 10 Praised, 11 Elm, 13 Permanent, 14 Calico, 16 Attend, 18 Endeavour, 20 Gem, 22 Drawled, 23 Sever, 25 Reassure, 26 Bath.
DOWN: 1 Halve, 2 Red, 4 Report, 5 Adamant, 6 Easter egg, 7 Sedated, 8 Weep, 12 Melodrama, 14 Cheddar, 15 Chablis, 17 Ponder, 19 Rose, 21 Mirth, 24 Via.

174
ACROSS: 1 Consent, 5 Rated, 8 Venue, 9 Novelty, 10 Newsagent, 12 Say, 13 Shindy, 14 Uphold, 17 Gas, 18 Quickness, 20 Raccoon, 21 Lupin, 23 Delve, 24 Witness.
DOWN: 1 Coven, 2 Nun, 3 Emerald, 4 Tinsel, 5 Rivet, 6 Telescope, 7 Dry-eyed, 11 Whimsical, 13 Sugared, 15 Pikelet, 16 Minnow, 18 Quote, 19 Sinus, 22 Pie.

175
ACROSS: 7 Weight, 8 Tebbit, 10 Against, 11 Arson, 12 Earl, 13 Order, 17 Doubt, 18 Germ, 22 Paint, 23 Trumpet, 24 Extend, 25 Assent.
DOWN: 1 Sweater, 2 Bizarre, 3 Shine, 4 Delayed, 5 Obese, 6 Stone, 9 Attribute, 14 Content, 15 Perplex, 16 Imitate, 19 Speed, 20 Ditto, 21 Purse.

176
ACROSS: 1 Gruesome, 7 Cedes, 8 Precipice, 9 Gnu, 10 Kiss, 11 Plaice, 13 Fellow, 14 Ulster, 17 Sailor, 18 Aden, 20 Rum, 22 Artichoke, 23 Small, 24 Princess.
DOWN: 1 Gopak, 2 Utensil, 3 Soil, 4 Mainly, 5 Adage, 6 Assurer, 7 Cedilla, 12 Logical, 13 Florist, 15 Tadpole, 16 Pooter, 17 Smear, 19 Needs, 21 Scan.

177
ACROSS: 7 Fought, 8 Knocks, 10 Embargo, 11 Equal, 12 Took, 13 Angst, 17 Fishy, 18 Zero, 22 Enter, 23 Nemesis, 24 Cerise, 25 Matron.
DOWN: 1 Effects, 2 Gumboot, 3 Charm, 4 Intense, 5 Scout, 6 Psalm, 9 Moonshine, 14 Digress, 15 Censure, 16 Godsend, 19 Ketch, 20 Stark, 21 Smear.

178
ACROSS: 1 Eyeful, 4 Tower, 8 Catch, 9 Idyllic, 10 Prepare, 11 Czar, 12 Tag, 14 Beta, 15 Itch, 18 Leo, 21 Halt, 23 Channel, 25 Stamina, 26 Theme, 27 Yield, 28 Ocelot.
DOWN: 1 Escape, 2 Extreme, 3 Upheaval, 4 Toys, 5 Waltz, 6 Record, 7 Tibet, 13 Gigantic, 16 Conceal, 17 Whisky, 19 Ocean, 20 Eldest, 22 Leave, 24 Wild.

179
ACROSS: 1 Chariot, 5 Tears, 8 Octet, 9 Gristle, 10 Defensive, 12 Irk, 13 Screed, 14 Argued, 17 Ape, 18 Guileless, 20 Pretext, 21 Idler, 23 Rated, 24 Regatta.
DOWN: 1 Crowd, 2 Act, 3 Intense, 4 Tigris, 5 Twine, 6 Attribute, 7 Sneaked, 11 Forcemeat, 13 Scarper, 15 Reeking, 16 Winter, 18 Greed, 19 Syria, 22 Lot.

180
ACROSS: 1 Chili, 4 Whether, 8 Scalpel, 9 Sixty, 10 Ideal, 11 Steeple, 13 Sway, 15 Rudder, 17 Kindle, 20 Even, 22 Condone, 24 Droop, 26 Wrest, 27 Taxable, 28 Runaway, 29 Dress.
DOWN: 1 Cashier, 2 Irate, 3 Impulse, 4 Walesa, 5 Ensue, 6 Hexapod, 7 Rhyme, 12 Tyke, 14 Wren, 16 Dungeon, 18 Indexed, 19 Express, 21 Vestry, 22 Cower, 23 On tow, 25 Ombre.

181 ───────
ACROSS:1 Dropping, 7 Align, 8 Vivacious, 9 Vow, 10 Tarn, 11 Alcove, 13 Vienna, 14 Anyhow, 17 Revive, 18 Agio, 20 Duo, 22 Recipient, 23 Kinky, 24 Sturgeon.
DOWN: 1 Divot, 2 Obverse, 3 Pack, 4 Noodle, 5 Sieve, 6 Know-how, 7 Astound, 12 Knavery, 13 Vandyke, 15 Hygiene, 16 Avocet, 17 Round, 19 Often, 21 Spar.

182 ───────
ACROSS:7 Higher, 8 Taller, 10 Agitate, 11 Empty, 12 Tier, 13 Guile, 17 Broth, 18 Robe, 22 Grain, 23 Nothing, 24 Easier, 25 Regret.
DOWN: 1 Chianti, 2 Ignited, 3 Decay, 4 Patella, 5 Slope, 6 Brays, 9 Reluctant, 14 Grandee, 15 Topiary, 16 Weighty, 19 Agree, 20 Pause, 21 Steep.

183 ───────
ACROSS:1 Colour, 4 Untie, 8 Odour, 9 Tighten, 10 Classic, 11 Alas, 12 Kin, 14 Odin, 15 Easy, 18 Gag, 21 Home, 23 Routine, 25 Sendoff, 26 On di, 27 Leeds, 28 Ostend.
DOWN: 1 Choice, 2 Leopard, 3 Uprising, 4 Urge, 5 Total, 6 Ernest, 7 Stock, 13 Nebulous, 16 Swindle, 17 Chisel, 19 Graft, 20 Pentad, 22 Manse, 24 Boss.

184 ───────
ACROSS:1 Brown, 4 Pastor, 9 Siamese, 10 Amass, 11 Omit, 12 Enhance, 13 Cur, 14 Juno, 16 Ibex, 18 Aid, 20 Placard, 21 Grip, 24 Eland, 25 Patella, 26 Dreary, 27 Mixed.
DOWN: 1 Boston, 2 Okapi, 3 Need, 5 Arachnid, 6 Trainee, 7 Rasher, 8 Sever, 13 Colander, 15 Unaware, 17 Upheld, 18 Adept, 19 Upland, 22 Relax, 23 Stem.

185 ───────
ACROSS:5 Write, 8 Reverend, 9 Smell, 10 Scramble, 11 Snare, 14 Cry, 16 Bureau, 17 Extent, 18 Met, 20 Lyons, 24 Applause, 25 Forge, 26 Intrepid, 27 Hydro.
DOWN: 1 Grasp, 2 Overt, 3 Cramp, 4 Angler, 6 Ruminate, 7 Tolerant, 12 Busybody, 13 Teenager, 14 Cum, 15 Yet, 19 Expand, 21 Glare, 22 Mumps, 23 Verdi.

186 ───────
ACROSS:1 Spring, 4 Bored, 8 River, 9 Fissure, 10 Fortune, 11 Mean, 12 Rap, 14 Mere, 15 Rose, 18 Dip, 21 Arch, 23 Riviera, 26 Convent, 26 Outer, 27 Ranch, 28 Ascend.
DOWN: 1 Strife, 2 Reverie, 3 Nurtured, 4 Bass, 5 Route, 6 Duenna, 7 After, 13 Previous, 16 Spectre, 17 Lascar, 19 Prate, 20 Barred, 22 Canon, 24 Mesh.

187 ───────
ACROSS:1 Pleas, 4 Academy, 8 Potency, 9 Optic, 10 Large, 11 Acrobat, 13 Rhyl, 15 Rodney, 17 Accent, 20 Dame, 22 Beloved, 24 Llama, 26 Revel, 27 Unicorn, 28 Harvest, 29 Style.
DOWN: 1 Popular, 2 Eater, 3 Sincere, 4 Anyway, 5 Amour, 6 Eatable, 7 Yacht, 12 Clam, 14 Hyde, 16 Deliver, 18 Celsius, 19 Trainee, 21 Adjust, 22 Birth, 23 Valve, 25 Agony.

188 ───────
ACROSS:1 Suite, 4 Torque, 9 Despair, 10 Guard, 11 Tune, 12 Minster, 13 Shy, 14 Grit, 16 Sure, 18 Ape, 20 Account, 21 Fete, 24 Bring, 25 Inspect, 26 Eleven, 27 Alter.
DOWN: 1 Sedate, 2 Ibsen, 3 Edam, 5 Organise, 6 Quarter, 7 Endure, 8 Grimy, 13 Struggle, 15 Recline, 17 Marble, 18 Attic, 19 Jester, 22 Erect, 23 Asia.

189 ───────
ACROSS:1 Freeze, 4 Peach, 8 Tulip, 9 Bravery, 10 Sapient, 11 Edge, 12 Elk, 14 Yeti, 15 Eddy, 18 Nap, 21 Rove, 23 Explode, 25 Sulphur, 26 Alert, 27 Rodeo, 28 Remedy.
DOWN: 1 Fetish, 2 Eclipse, 3 Zeppelin, 4 Play, 5 Ahead, 6 Hoyden, 7 Abate, 13 Keepsake, 16 Diocese, 17 Eraser, 19 Pearl, 20 Sentry, 22 Valid, 24 Ohio.

190 ───────
ACROSS:1 House, 4 Guessed, 8 Dwindle, 9 Actor, 10 Layer, 11 Isolate, 13 Sect, 15 Outlet, 17 Accent, 20 Orgy, 22 Cologne, 24 Circa, 26 Stiff, 27 Knossos, 28 Discern, 29 Epsom.
DOWN: 1 Hidalgo, 2 Unify, 3 Endorse, 4 Gaelic, 5 Erato, 6 Situate, 7 Dirge, 12 Stag, 14 Eton, 16 Tallies, 18 Cyclone, 19 Transom, 21 Reckon, 22 Cased, 23 Gaffe, 25 Risks.

191 ————
ACROSS:1 Meatier, 5 Rites, 8 Girth, 9 Matelot, 10 Control, 11 Impel, 12 Greedy, 14 Hangar, 17 Zippy, 19 Tornado, 22 Lottery, 23 Alien, 24 Ethos, 25 Remorse.
DOWN: 1 Magic, 2 Arrange, 3 Ichor, 4 Rumble, 5 Retsina, 6 Tulip, 7 Settler, 12 Gazelle, 13 Dryness, 15 Glacier, 16 Stayer, 18 Patch, 20 Realm, 21 Ounce.

192 ————
ACROSS:7 Butter, 8 Moment, 10 Neglect, 11 Noose, 12 Owns, 13 Truck, 17 Filly, 18 Tyre, 22 Blunt, 23 Sardine, 24 Splint, 25 Morass.
DOWN: 1 Abandon, 2 Staging, 3 Deter, 4 Connect, 5 Felon, 6 Steed, 9 Sterilise, 14 Sitting, 15 Cynical, 16 Decease, 19 Abuse, 20 Bully, 21 Brood.

193 ————
ACROSS:1 Rode, 3 Sweeping, 9 Venom, 10 Gnocchi, 11 Lap, 13 Gravesend, 14 Creamy, 16 Athene, 18 Practical, 20 Tup, 22 Treadle, 23 Novel, 25 Literati, 26 Styx.
DOWN: 1 Rival, 2 Den, 4 Wigwam, 5 Erodent, 6 Increment, 7 Griddle, 8 Smug, 12 Prevalent, 14 Capital, 15 Matador, 17 Accept, 19 Lynx, 21 Phlox, 24 Vet.

194 ————
ACROSS:1 Fosse, 4 Hills, 10 Recover, 11 Awful, 12 Error, 13 Detroit, 15 Aged, 17 Smile, 19 Gaffe, 22 Reed, 25 Dilemma, 27 Argue, 29 Inter, 30 Examine, 31 Haven, 32 Otter.
DOWN: 2 Occur, 3 Several, 5 Inapt, 6 Lift-off, 7 Brief, 8 Pride, 9 Flute, 14 Edge, 16 Germ, 18 Militia, 20 Adamant, 21 Admit, 23 Eager, 24 Sever, 26 Merge, 28 Guide.

195 ————
ACROSS:1 Sarah, 4 Neighed, 8 Doormat, 9 Bully, 10 Cabot, 11 Overbid, 13 Erne, 15 Retire, 17 Arctic, 20 Solo, 22 Flighty, 24 Sepia, 26 Uvula, 27 Torment, 28 Elector, 29 Minor.
DOWN: 1 Sidecar, 2 Rhomb, 3 Hamster, 4 Notion, 5 Imbue, 6 Halibut, 7 Dryad, 12 Veal, 14 Rest, 16 Tribute, 18 Rostrum, 19 Chatter, 21 Oyster, 22 Fluke, 23 Heart, 25 Preen.

196 ————
ACROSS:1 Cooker, 4 Dinner, 7 Fruitless, 9 Lard, 10 Etch, 11 Dinar, 13 Renown, 14 Seated, 15 Finals, 17 Geisha, 19 Total, 20 Last, 22 Lair, 23 Seclusion, 24 Warmed, 25 Digest.
DOWN: 1 Cellar, 2 Kurd, 3 Raisin, 4 Dallas, 5 Nose, 6 Rushed, 7 Frankness, 8 Statesman, 11 Dwelt, 12 Rebel, 15 Fallow, 16 Soiled, 17 Gassed, 18 Abrupt, 21 Term, 22 Long.

197 ————
ACROSS:1 Jewel, 4 Control, 8 Release, 9 Gulls, 10 Casts, 11 Isthmus, 13 Oath, 15 Oblong, 17 Output, 20 Even, 22 Collide, 24 Dream, 26 Miami, 27 Special, 28 Crystal, 29 Satyr.
DOWN: 1 Jericho, 2 Wells, 3 Liaison, 4 Credit, 5 Night, 6 Rollmop, 7 Lasts, 12 Shoe, 14 Aged, 16 Lullaby, 18 Undress, 19 Tumbler, 21 Vessel, 22 Comic, 23 Idiot, 25 Edict.

198 ————
ACROSS:1 Shops, 4 Oiled, 10 Connote, 11 Tudor, 12 Truce, 13 Ceramic, 15 Idea, 17 Atone, 19 Smack, 22 Note, 25 Canasta, 27 Doubt, 29 Peril, 30 Incline, 31 Smirk, 32 Fleet.
DOWN: 2 Hindu, 3 Protein, 5 Inter, 6 Endemic, 7 Scott, 8 Peace, 9 Crack, 14 East, 16 Dent, 18 Tantrum, 20 Medical, 21 Scope, 23 Oasis, 24 Steep, 26 Solar, 28 Unite.

199 ————
ACROSS:1 Strait, 4 Aweigh, 7 Indignant, 9 Mine, 10 Erin, 11 Bleak, 13 Toupee, 14 Liquid, 15 Plinth, 17 Strand, 19 Holly, 20 Blur, 22 Bias, 23 Soporific, 24 Copper, 25 Hidden.
DOWN: 1 Submit, 2 Acne, 3 Trifle, 4 Annual, 5 Erne, 6 Horned, 7 Injurious, 8 Traumatic, 11 Berth, 12 Kitty, 15 Public, 16 Honour, 17 Sleigh, 18 Design, 21 Romp, 22 Bind.

200 ————
ACROSS:1 Farther, 5 Thyme, 8 Riper, 9 Compute, 10 Eternal, 11 Ochre, 12 Siesta, 14 Mallet, 17 Again, 19 Liberty, 22 Surpass, 23 Obese, 24 Amend, 25 Samoyed.
DOWN: 1 Force, 2 Replete, 3 Heron, 4 Recall, 5 Tombola, 6 Youth, 7 Everest, 12 Swansea, 13 Tankard, 15 Larceny, 16 Closes, 18 Agree, 20 Bloom, 21 Yield.

201
ACROSS:7 League, **8** Allies, **10** Message, **11** Natal, **12** Enow, **13** Haven, **17** Rabid, **18** Smug, **22** Tulip, **23** Unearth, **24** Maroon, **25** Odessa.
DOWN: 1 Climber, **2** Mansion, **3** Lunar, **4** Flunkey, **5** Pinto, **6** Psalm, **9** Tenacious, **14** Harpoon, **15** Impress, **16** Egghead, **19** Stump, **20** Flare, **21** Ready.

202
ACROSS:1 Hoyden, **4** Sikhs, **8** Agree, **9** Erudite, **10** Swished, **11** Zeal, **12** Odd, **14** Stun, **15** Imam, **18** Tip, **21** Ache, **23** Leprosy, **25** Torment, **26** Troth, **27** Loyal, **28** Chaser.
DOWN: 1 Hearse, **2** Yorkist, **3** Elephant, **4** Smug, **5** Knife, **6** Seemly, **7** Kendo, **13** Dispatch, **16** Amorous, **17** Pastel, **19** Pluto, **20** Cypher, **22** Harpy, **24** Fell.

203
ACROSS:1 Defence, **5** Sieve, **8** Venal, **9** Publish, **10** Thinner, **11** Again, **12** Rugged, **14** Chance, **17** Comet, **19** Pierrot, **22** Chianti, **23** Growl, **24** Elect, **25** Gherkin.
DOWN: 1 Duvet, **2** Fencing, **3** Nylon, **4** Expert, **5** Sabbath, **6** Erica, **7** Enhance, **12** Recycle, **13** Extinct, **15** Norfolk, **16** Spring, **18** Maize, **20** Eagle, **21** Talon.

204
ACROSS:5 Notts, **8** Apprised, **9** Tempo, **10** Fraction, **11** Berry, **14** Pet, **16** Urbane, **17** Ostend, **18** Pan, **20** Again, **24** Conceive, **25** Visor, **26** Pinnacle, **27** Study.
DOWN: 1 Banff, **2** Sprat, **3** Firth, **4** Remote, **6** Omelette, **7** Tapering, **12** Druggist, **13** Manifold, **14** Pep, **15** Ton, **19** Adonis, **21** Scant, **22** Pitch, **23** Betel.

205
ACROSS:1 Peter, **4** Doubt, **10** Redress, **11** Razor, **12** Corgi, **13** Abscond, **15** Ably, **17** Brace, **19** Rabat, **22** Skew, **25** Modiste, **27** Kebab, **29** Lucky, **30** Granite, **31** Idiot, **32** Added.
DOWN: 2 Elder, **3** Elegiac, **5** Orris, **6** Bazooka, **7** Crick, **8** Usual, **9** Pride, **14** Byre, **16** Best, **18** Reduced, **20** Awkward, **21** Amble, **23** Kedge, **24** Abbey, **26** Say-so, **28** Bride.

206
ACROSS:1 Calmer, **4** Light, **8** Erase, **9** Amateur, **10** Rancher, **11** Idle, **12** Yap, **14** Eden, **15** Rock, **18** Tip, **21** Asks, **23** Explain, **25** Present, **26** Erode, **27** Rider, **28** Cyprus.
DOWN: 1 Cherry, **2** Learned, **3** Elephant, **4** Load, **5** Greed, **6** Tureen, **7** Carry, **13** Prophesy, **16** Clamour, **17** Tamper, **19** Petty, **20** Enters, **22** Knead, **24** Rear.

207
ACROSS:1 Please, **4** Argent, **7** Compliant, **9** Darn, **10** Gasp, **11** Trout, **13** Report, **14** Simper, **15** Polish, **17** Minute, **19** Tepid, **20** Bank, **22** Dive, **23** Tragedian, **24** Crisis, **25** Yonder.
DOWN: 1 Ponder, **2** Anon, **3** Expert, **4** Animus, **5** Gong, **6** Tamper, **7** Crapulent, **8** Tarpaulin, **11** Trust, **12** Timid, **15** Public, **16** Hedges, **17** Midday, **18** Exeter, **21** Kris, **22** Dawn.

208
ACROSS:1 Chain, **4** Sores, **10** Trapper, **11** Tiger, **12** Usher, **13** Dickens, **15** Icon, **17** Idyll, **19** Caddy, **22** Agar, **25** Dentine, **27** Cabal, **29** Pasha, **30** Sheriff, **31** Cynic, **32** Lying.
DOWN: 2 Heath, **3** Imperil, **5** Optic, **6** Egghead, **7** Strut, **8** Credo, **9** Crass, **14** Inca, **16** Clan, **18** Dynasty, **20** Archery, **21** Adept, **23** Gesso, **24** Bluff, **26** Iraqi, **28** Bairn.

209
ACROSS:7 Terror, **8** Wrists, **10** Mammoth, **11** Cheer, **12** Nook, **13** Brief, **17** Mouse, **18** Well, **22** Hiker, **23** Uncover, **24** Melody, **25** Tennis.
DOWN: 1 Stamina, **2** Crimson, **3** Colon, **4** Proceed, **5** Aspen, **6** Usurp, **9** Shares out, **14** Comrade, **15** Leaving, **16** Florist, **19** Theme, **20** Skill, **21** Octet.

210
ACROSS:1 Maker, **4** Bloomer, **8** Grandee, **9** Handy, **10** Anise, **11** Operate, **13** Sane, **15** Thrust, **17** Street, **20** Oboe, **22** Welcome, **24** Talon, **26** Erase, **27** Kinsman, **28** Tweeter, **29** Sandy.
DOWN: 1 Migrant, **2** Khaki, **3** Redress, **4** Breton, **5** Ochre, **6** Mundane, **7** Rhyme, **12** Peso, **14** Atom, **16** Release, **18** Tetanus, **19** Tenancy, **21** Beaker, **22** Wrest, **23** Overt, **25** Lemon.

211 ―――――

ACROSS:5 Jerry, **8** Mandarin, **9** Spade, **10** Carapace, **11** Ideal, **14** Ass, **16** Vertex, **17** Tattoo, **18** Ely, **20** Stick, **24** Exterior, **25** Scamp, **26** Straddle, **27** Slant.
DOWN: 1 Smock, **2** Snort, **3** Happy, **4** Pisces, **6** Expedite, **7** Radiator, **12** Vertical, **13** Stockman, **14** Axe, **15** Sty, **19** Laxity, **21** Pedal, **22** Wilde, **23** Cruet.

212 ―――――

ACROSS:1 Consort, **5** Hauls, **8** Atlas, **9** Ammeter, **10** Encounter, **12** Run, **13** Singer, **14** Strove, **17** Roe, **18** Barometer, **20** Endless, **21** Eaten, **23** Tired, **24** Outcome.
DOWN: 1 Cease, **2** Nil, **3** Obscure, **4** Traits, **5** Homer, **6** Uttermost, **7** Strange, **11** Contender, **13** Serpent, **15** Tempest, **16** Fresco, **18** Blend, **19** Rinse, **22** Two.

213 ―――――

ACROSS:1 Knights, **5** Cools, **8** Doyen, **9** Torpedo, **10** Streamlet, **12** Irk, **13** Decide, **14** Manner, **17** Ill, **18** Somnolent, **20** Dredger, **21** Award, **23** Extra, **24** Economy.
DOWN: 1 Kudos, **2** Icy, **3** Hansard, **4** Settle, **5** Carat, **6** Obedience, **7** Snooker, **11** Recollect, **13** Dwindle, **15** Avocado, **16** Emerge, **18** Sigma, **19** Toddy, **22** Ado.

214 ―――――

ACROSS:1 Cereal, **4** Rites, **8** Upset, **9** Hastily, **10** Cadaver, **11** Mesh, **12** Pub, **14** Hess, **15** Erse, **18** Tau, **21** Avid, **23** Tighten, **25** Beguile, **26** Abhor, **27** Extol, **28** Medley.
DOWN: 1 Church, **2** Residue, **3** Activist, **4** Rash, **5** Trite, **6** Scythe, **7** Sharp, **13** Belgrade, **16** Satchel, **17** Gamble, **19** Utter, **20** Energy, **22** Ingot, **24** Will.

215 ―――――

ACROSS:1 Agree, **4** Phobia, **9** Whisper, **10** Trust, **11** Yank, **12** Perfume, **13** Wye, **14** Rhea, **16** City, **18** Ask, **20** Surfeit, **21** Oral, **24** Frill, **25** Avocado, **26** Lagoon, **27** Egypt.
DOWN: 1 Always, **2** Reign, **3** Espy, **5** Hat-trick, **6** Bouquet, **7** Anthem, **8** Grape, **13** Waterloo, **15** Herring, **17** Useful, **18** Atlas, **19** Almost, **22** Ready, **23** Rome.

216 ―――――

ACROSS:5 Belle, **8** Wringing, **9** Bitch, **10** Uncooked, **11** Stout, **14** Sty, **16** Chrome, **17** Evoked, **18** Art, **20** Bumph, **24** Stallion, **25** Idols, **26** Pedicure, **27** Prude.
DOWN: 1 Awful, **2** Witch, **3** Igloo, **4** Invest, **6** Eviction, **7** Lectured, **12** Shoulder, **13** Compiled, **14** Sea, **15** Yet, **19** Rotter, **21** Flail, **22** Virus, **23** Enter.

217 ―――――

ACROSS:1 Trance, **4** Sacked, **7** Amorphous, **9** Club, **10** Mask, **11** Snoop, **13** Rioted, **14** Ladder, **15** Uproar, **17** Zenith, **19** Nadir, **20** Rapt, **22** Hemp, **23** Harbinger, **24** Tingle, **25** Append.
DOWN: 1 Tracer, **2** Numb, **3** Errand, **4** School, **5** Chum, **6** Docker, **7** Autograph, **8** Sandpiper, **11** Sedan, **12** Pater, **15** Uproot, **16** Rabble, **17** Zinnia, **18** Hopped, **21** Tang, **22** Help.

218 ―――――

ACROSS:7 Billow, **8** Stares, **10** Outside, **11** Drama, **12** View, **13** Piano, **17** Drink, **18** Face, **22** Round, **23** Nothing, **24** Create, **25** Blonde.
DOWN: 1 Absolve, **2** Clothed, **3** Logic, **4** Student, **5** Broad, **6** Oscar, **9** Beginning, **14** Erudite, **15** Radiant, **16** Feigned, **19** Brace, **20** Quiet, **21** Stalk.

219 ―――――

ACROSS:1 Chancery, **7** Marks, **8** Overstate, **9** Pit, **10** Drop, **11** Hornet, **13** Cheeky, **14** Jersey, **17** Untrue, **18** Exit, **20** Cup, **22** Hermitage, **23** Enemy, **24** Educated.
DOWN: 1 Crowd, **2** Anemone, **3** Cask, **4** Reason, **5** Crypt, **6** Ashtray, **7** Meander, **12** Sketchy, **13** Cricket, **15** Sextant, **16** Putrid, **17** Upset, **19** Tweed, **21** Zinc.

220 ―――――

ACROSS:5 Piece, **8** Treaties, **9** Using, **10** Indecent, **11** Impel, **14** Cry, **16** Angora, **17** Aviary, **18** Map, **20** Curse, **24** Scimitar, **25** Stoop, **26** Entrance, **27** Gypsy.
DOWN: 1 Attic, **2** Veldt, **3** Stock, **4** Keener, **6** Insomnia, **7** Canberra, **12** Industry, **13** Couscous, **14** Cam, **15** Yap, **19** Arcane, **21** Smirk, **22** Stunt, **23** Creel.

221 ——————

ACROSS:1 Cleans, **4** Haven, **8** Churn, **9** Fatigue, **10** Example, **11** Snub, **12** New, **14** Tern, **15** Espy, **18** Sap, **21** Echo, **23** Lugworm, **25** Monsoon, **26** Offal, **27** Noyes, **28** Adored.
DOWN:1 Cycles, **2** Emulate, **3** Ninepins, **4** Hate, **5** Vegan, **6** Need-be, **7** Often, **13** Wedgwood, **16** Proffer, **17** Sermon, **19** Plonk, **20** Smiled, **22** Honey, **24** Boss.

222 ——————

ACROSS:1 Broker, **4** Bottle, **7** Snowstorm, **9** Twit, **10** Tyre, **11** Drill, **13** Candid, **14** Easter, **15** Retail, **17** Pilfer, **19** Titan, **20** Guru, **22** Heat, **23** Enchained, **24** Newton, **25** Gallon.
DOWN:1 Baltic, **2** Kent, **3** Reward, **4** Battle, **5** Tart, **6** Endear, **7** Signature, **8** Mystified, **11** Digit, **12** Latin, **15** Raglan, **16** Lichen, **17** Paling, **18** Rotten, **21** Unit, **22** Heal.

223 ——————

ACROSS:1 Astra, **4** Noughts, **8** Concord, **9** Tasty, **10** Hasty, **11** Foliage, **13** Tuft, **15** Lather, **17** Impend, **20** Dace, **22** Harmful, **24** Licit, **26** Rhino, **27** Godetia, **28** Eminent, **29** Caret.
DOWN:1 Alcohol, **2** Tunis, **3** Acolyte, **4** Nod off, **5** Until, **6** Hostage, **7** Style, **12** Otic, **14** Urdu, **16** Termini, **18** Melodic, **19** Detract, **21** Alight, **22** Horde, **23** Frome, **25** Cater.

224 ——————

ACROSS:1 Check, **4** Cough, **10** Avarice, **11** Senna, **12** Laden, **13** Ostrich, **15** Tint, **17** Rapid, **19** Order, **22** Lope, **25** Terrier, **27** Ledge, **29** Cadge, **30** Trainee, **31** Realm, **32** Heart.
DOWN:2 Hoard, **3** Chianti, **5** Onset, **6** Genuine, **7** Eagle, **8** Demon, **9** Yacht, **14** Stop, **16** Idle, **18** Abridge, **20** Release, **21** Stick, **23** Orate, **24** Never, **26** Ideal, **28** Donor.

225 ——————

ACROSS:1 Beech, **4** Coaming, **8** Leeward, **9** Grebe, **10** Noyes, **11** Linctus, **13** Abet, **15** Embryo, **17** Crease, **20** Soho, **22** Jujitsu, **24** Mauve, **26** Cowes, **27** Canasta, **28** Balcony, **29** Acted.
DOWN:1 Balance, **2** Enemy, **3** Hearsay, **4** Coddle, **5** Argon, **6** Inertia, **7** Guess, **12** Itch, **14** Boss, **16** Bejewel, **18** Romania, **19** Emerald, **21** Outcry, **22** Jacob, **23** Tasso, **25** Upset.

226 ——————

ACROSS:1 Pitcher, **5** Cards, **8** Lhasa, **9** Gentile, **10** Foolhardy, **12** Apt, **13** Casino, **14** Zodiac, **17** Bus, **18** Semblance, **20** Climate, **21** Adieu, **23** Ennui, **24** Essence.
DOWN:1 Pilaf, **2** Tea, **3** Heathen, **4** Regard, **5** Canny, **6** Ruination, **7** Sceptic, **11** Obsession, **13** Cubicle, **15** Orleans, **16** Impede, **18** Swami, **19** Etude, **22** Inn.

227 ——————

ACROSS:1 Question, **7** Heirs, **8** Expensive, **9** Lah, **10** Loom, **11** Starve, **13** Hasten, **14** Carpet, **17** Season, **18** Arid, **20** Bee, **22** Sanctuary, **23** Ranee, **24** Parmesan.
DOWN:1 Quell, **2** Employs, **3** Tiny, **4** Opiate, **5** Lisle, **6** Asphalt, **7** Hearsay, **12** Because, **13** Hamburg, **15** Perhaps, **16** Cornea, **17** Seine, **19** Doyen, **21** Stem.

228 ——————

ACROSS:1 Sauce, **4** Error, **10** Protect, **11** Vetch, **12** Curio, **13** Lardoon, **15** Open, **17** Flute, **19** Tenet, **22** Apex, **25** Thimble, **27** Terse, **29** Gauge, **30** Clutter, **31** Petty, **32** Beard.
DOWN:2 Amour, **3** Cheroot, **5** Rover, **6** Outcome, **7** Spice, **8** Stale, **9** Think, **14** Ante, **16** Peal, **18** Leisure, **20** Extrude, **21** Stage, **23** Peach, **24** Ferry, **26** Bleat, **28** Rotor.

229 ——————

ACROSS:1 Chilli, **4** Source, **7** Quadruped, **9** Tour, **10** Dido, **11** Snick, **13** Single, **14** Enacts, **15** Nausea, **17** Salver, **19** Plaid, **20** Mule, **22** Aria, **23** Extremity, **24** Dictum, **25** Rumour.
DOWN:1 Cactus, **2** Lour, **3** Iodine, **4** Sluice, **5** Used, **6** Emboss, **7** Quintuple, **8** Discovery, **11** Sleep, **12** Knead, **15** Nimrod, **16** Alarum, **17** Simmer, **18** Reaper, **21** Exit, **22** Atom.

230 ——————

ACROSS:1 Lank, **3** Ayrshire, **9** Title, **10** Abusive, **11** Run, **13** Reluctant, **14** Cygnet, **16** Unwind, **18** Stiffness, **20** Get, **22** Averred, **23** Grain, **25** Detested, **26** Mere.
DOWN:1 Later, **2** Net, **4** Yearly, **5** Soupcon, **6** Imitating, **7** Elected, **8** Dear, **12** Negligent, **14** Custard, **15** Efforts, **17** Meddle, **19** Sign, **21** Tense, **24** Ale.

231 ────────
ACROSS:5 Greta, 8 Traction, 9 Adept, 10 Abstruse, 11 Otter, 14 Sty, 16 Fibula, 17 Arrive, 18 Dip, 20 Pitch, 24 Applause, 25 Magma, 26 Adhesive, 27 Stork.
DOWN: 1 Steal, 2 False, 3 Stern, 4 Cosset, 6 Redstart, 7 Top-heavy, 12 Vigilant, 13 Dulcimer, 14 Sad, 15 Yap, 19 Impede, 21 Fleet, 22 Lurid, 23 Defer.

232 ────────
ACROSS:1 Fighter, 5 Plain, 8 Badge, 9 Cardiac, 10 Elevate, 11 Lance, 12 Mascot, 14 Oxygen, 17 Risky, 19 Orderly, 22 Amnesia, 23 Omaha, 24 Amity, 25 Express.
DOWN: 1 Fable, 2 Godless, 3 Theta, 4 Racket, 5 Perplex, 6 Alien, 7 Nucleon, 12 Marsala, 13 Odyssey, 15 Garbage, 16 Homage, 18 Sinai, 20 Droop, 21 Yeats.

233 ────────
ACROSS:5 Sport, 8 Sedition, 9 Truth, 10 Lipstick, 11 Chick, 14 Arc, 16 Fabric, 17 Result, 18 Toy, 20 Raise, 24 Adjacent, 25 Court, 26 Tapestry, 27 Hades.
DOWN: 1 Psalm, 2 Adept, 3 State, 4 Concur, 6 Purchase, 7 Reticule, 12 Casanova, 13 Preserve, 14 Act, 15 Cry, 19 Old-hat, 21 Label, 22 Jetty, 23 Stays.

234 ────────
ACROSS:1 Floating, 7 Alone, 8 Transient, 9 Son, 10 Heil, 11 Serene, 13 Confer, 14 Spider, 17 Opting, 18 Abed, 20 Paw, 22 Realistic, 23 Emend, 24 Deterred.
DOWN: 1 Fetch, 2 Ovation, 3 Tass, 4 Nieces, 5 Morse, 6 Meander, 7 Attempt, 12 Leotard, 13 Complex, 15 Debater, 16 Engage, 17 Owned, 19 Diced, 21 Dive.

235 ────────
ACROSS:1 Straight, 7 Laced, 8 Retaliate, 9 Imp, 10 Puny, 11 Staked, 13 Shandy, 14 Agreed, 17 Fresco, 18 Wilt, 20 Mar, 22 Squeamish, 23 Slime, 24 Clarence.
DOWN: 1 Strop, 2 Rotunda, 3 Idly, 4 Health, 5 Acrid, 6 Adapted, 7 Leakage, 12 Adverse, 13 Surmise, 15 Edition, 16 Actual, 17 Frail, 19 Tehee, 21 Fair.

236 ────────
ACROSS:1 Shore, 4 Enough, 9 Rhizome, 10 Anger, 11 Same, 12 Bonanza, 13 Lay, 14 Magi, 16 Soya, 18 Ass, 20 Enamels, 21 Fear, 24 Obese, 25 Anguish, 26 Purist, 27 Yearn.
DOWN: 1 Stress, 2 Odium, 3 Eros, 5 Nearness, 6 Urgency, 7 Herbal, 8 Derby, 13 Lifeless, 15 Amateur, 17 Recoup, 18 Aswan, 19 Orphan, 22 Erica, 23 Ugly.

237 ────────
ACROSS:7 Strike, 8 Accord, 10 Roister, 11 Atoll, 12 Dolt, 13 Steed, 17 Stern, 18 Wash, 22 Laser, 23 Trident, 24 Arable, 25 Fiance.
DOWN: 1 Astride, 2 Braille, 3 Skate, 4 Scraped, 5 Moron, 6 Adult, 9 Preterite, 14 Startle, 15 Cayenne, 16 Chatter, 19 Bleat, 20 Oscar, 21 Pixie.

238 ────────
ACROSS:1 Shortest, 7 Roots, 8 Interfere, 9 Goa, 10 Teak, 11 Attire, 13 Mutiny, 14 Cerise, 17 Aghast, 18 Spur, 20 Sot, 22 Nefarious, 23 Valet, 24 Flawless.
DOWN: 1 Shift, 2 Outcast, 3 Tarn, 4 Sheath, 5 Forge, 6 Escapee, 7 Refined, 12 Enchant, 13 Missive, 15 Implore, 16 Useful, 17 Atoll, 19 Risks, 21 Draw.

239 ────────
ACROSS:1 Caught, 4 Arise, 8 Amass, 9 Release, 10 Gravest, 11 Cede, 12 Hot, 14 Mere, 15 Over, 18 Din, 21 Task, 23 Elector, 25 Imitate, 26 Ahead, 27 Enter, 28 Kettle.
DOWN: 1 Change, 2 Unaware, 3 Hastened, 4 Ally, 5 Inane, 6 Eleven, 7 Broth, 13 Tolerate, 16 Entreat, 17 Strive, 19 Never, 20 Bridge, 22 Swift, 24 Fair.

240 ────────
ACROSS:1 Grass, 4 Routes, 9 Realism, 10 Tinge, 11 Lode, 12 Scourge, 13 Ass, 14 Bard, 16 Some, 18 Are, 20 Compact, 21 Tool, 24 Range, 25 Ancient, 26 Errata, 27 Ranch.
DOWN: 1 Gargle, 2 Award, 3 Suit, 5 Outhouse, 6 Tantrum, 7 Shekel, 8 Amass, 13 Adjacent, 15 Almoner, 17 Scarce, 18 Atlas, 19 Clutch, 22 Ocean, 23 Acer.